Exploring the
Oregon Coast
by Car

Exploring the
Oregon Coast
by Car

A Guide to Special Places & Activities

Marje Blood

IMAGE IMPRINTS
P.O. Box 2764
Eugene, OR 97402

Library of Congress Cataloging in Publication Data

Blood, Marje
  Exploring the Oregon Coast by Car.

  Includes index.
  1. Oregon—Description and travel—1951—Guide-books.
  2. Automobiles—Road guides—Oregon.
I. Title
F874.3.B56 1980   917.95'0433   80-25484
ISBN 0-9615233-3-6
Library of Congress Number: 85-81529

Second Edition - 1986

Published by   Image Imprints
               P.O. Box 2764
               Eugene, Oregon 97402

First Edition Published 1980
2nd Printing 1981
Update Printing 1983 by The Writing Works, Seattle WA
Published in Canada 1980 by Gordon Soules Book Co.,
                              Vancouver, BC Canada

ACKNOWLEDGMENTS

My grateful thanks goes to these people who helped me see this book through to completion: Sylvia and Jerry Towne, Val Thoenig, Kim Hill, Jim and June White, Ione Reed, Mary Lou Skinner, Renny Strahota; and especially to Mimi Bell.

Photo Credits

Cover, Waterfront at Newport by Anne Hinds, 98; Mimi Bell, 51, 78; Marj Jorgensen, 109, 132 (bottom); Mary Jean Kelso, 176; Karen Kneaper, 110; Oregon State Travel Department, 36, 59; Ione Reed, 7, 23, 31, 157, 175; Ward Robertson, 168; James Seeley White, 2, 20, 27, 34, 45, 47, 53; Doug Wilson, 150; all others by Marje Blood.

Contents

Foreword   vii

Exploring the Oregon Coast by Car   1

The Corps of Discovery   5

Section 1: Astoria, Warrenton, Seaside,
           Cannon Beach   11

The Lighthouses   37

Section II: Tillamook, Nehalem   43

The Whales   57

Section III: Lincoln City, Depoe Bay   61

The Indians   79

Section IV: Newport, Waldport   83

The Dunes   99

Section V: Yachats, Florence, Reedsport   103

The Bridges   133

Section VI: North Bend, Coos Bay, Charleston   137

Catching More Bottom Fish   151

Section VII: Bandon, Port Orford   155

Sea Explorers of the Oregon Coast   177

Section VIII: Gold Beach, Brookings   183

Events Calendar   207

Index   209

Foreword

Appropriately Marje Blood begins her book with a review of that famed expedition across the continent to the Oregon coast by Lewis and Clark's "Corps of Discovery" nearly 200 years ago. Her own exploration by car is a small tour of discovery in itself. From the mouth of the Columbia River to the California border, she has discovered the *specials*, the exciting surprises, the off-beat nooks and crannies that a woman with imagination and unending curiosity does find.

She takes us to meet the artists and craftsmen who work to the rhythms of the sea in glass and wood and clay and gems gathered from the sand. She discovers the nostalgic and the new, she tells us about those first dauntless adventurers who came by sailing ship, and about how modern machines whisk cranberries out of seashore bogs. She finds magic in a toy factory and excitement in swooshing up and down the sand dunes of Oregon's own Sahara, and she directs us to the best clam chowder, the most special scampi, and the freshest coffee on the route. Much more than a guide, her book is a celebration of the lovely Oregon Coast.

MIMI BELL

v

Exploring the Oregon Coast by Car

This is a book about some special places on the Oregon Coast. It's not about the "best" places, nor the "most popular" ones, nor about the "most unusual." And not all of the special places are included. The ones I've written about are those that, for one reason or another, seemed to belong in the book I wanted to write.

Exploring the Oregon Coast by Car isn't a traditional guidebook, although it can be used as such. It has more writing than most guide books—stories about interesting places and people and events that too often get lost in the shuffle in travel guides.

I decided I'd write a "nooks and crannies" guidebook; one that would accommodate changing patterns in vacation and recreation travel. This book is composed of eight sections, each focusing on a specific coastal area. Within each division, the attractions which make that region unique are featured. These sections are separated by general articles that pertain to the Oregon coast as a whole. In effect, the book comprises a series of regional magazines, bound together to form a book covering the 390-mile Oregon coastline.

1

Misty Neahkahnie Mountain, viewed across Nehalem Bay, was considered by the Indians to be a dwelling place of coyote god Talapus.

I began by concentrating on small places, visiting with shop owners, artists, and craftspeople who work and live along Oregon's Pacific boundary—and looked for places often by-passed by travelers. But it soon became obvious that it would be all but impossible to write a guide without including those places that have become landmarks over the years. I could never explain an Oregon Coast guide without stories about **Sea Lion Caves**, for instance, or **Bruce's Candy Kitchen**.

Instead I tried to see these veteran attractions from a new perspective via personal interviews and experiences. As the bits and pieces of familiar detail interwove with new information, a total picture of Oregon's magnificent coast began to emerge, reflecting a region of natural beauty and fulfilling life styles unique to this country, and perhaps in the world.

Many special places are not included in this book. In every case I have tried to select a cross section of attractions which, taken together, would be representative of the area, and interesting enough to draw visitors to the locality to explore further for themselves. I know the others exist. If your special place has not been profiled in these pages, I'm sorry. I hope you'll enjoy mine.

Beverly Beach seven miles north of Newport has an awesome collection of driftwood. The state park, one of several which offer year-around camping, has 150 sites, more than 100 trailer sites, plus picnic facilities. Additional recreational accommodations include a utility building and a theater.

The Corps of Discovery

The expedition commissioned by President Thomas Jefferson under the leadership of Army Captain Meriwether Lewis and William Clark was one of the most ambitious voyages of exploration in the history of the United States. Jefferson's general commission to map the virgin wilderness routes also included explicit instructions to follow the rivers flowing west above the Missouri River system in search of the fabled Northwest Passage. The diaries kept by the two men comply in minute detail with his further instructions to record their observations of natural history, botanical and zoological information, and the appearance and customs of the native peoples they encountered along the way.

The 45 men departed St. Louis without fanfare on May 14, 1804, and for five months worked their way upstream 1,600 miles to the Mandan villages in the Dakota territory, where they wintered in Fort Mandan, constructed by the party near the Indian villages. This neighborliness during the long winter months caused the leaders some concern over their men fraternizing with the attractive Mandan women.

In April of 1805, having engaged the services of Toussaint Charboneau and his young Shoshone wife Sacajawea as interpreters and guides, the party—now down to 29 members—spent the summer crossing the continental divide and on August 11 made contact with the Shoshones. Caching their canoes by filling them with rocks and sinking them in the river, they bought horses from relatives of Sacajawea and pushed ahead, anxious to finish the mountain crossings before the winter snows.

Near the end of September Nez Perce on the Clearwater River affirmed that the Columbia River would take them to the Pacific. Building canoes of cedar and leaving their horses with the Indians, the party began the final leg of the journey. On November 7 Clark recorded they had sighted the ocean, and on December 3 carved his name and the date into a pine tree overlooking the Pacific on the north side of the Columbia.

For 10 days, battered by winds and tides which set their camp in a small cove afloat, the leaders observed the natives crossing the stormy bay in their canoes in spite of mountainous tides. Believing the south side of the river offered a better site for a winter stay, the company took advantage of a brief clearing spell to make the crossing themselves.

Three miles up the river now named for them, Lewis and Clark began to build their winter quarters of logs and shingles in pouring rain which seldom let up, and then for only a few hours at a time. By Christmas they were under cover and trading with nearby Indians. Fort Clatsop was named after the most attractive of the nearby tribes, the Clatsops, who were a source of help during the remainder of the stay.

They spent the winter drying elk meat, making clothes to replace their rotting buckskins, tanning skins of smaller animals for blankets, and refining salt upon the cairn set up at the beach 15 miles to the south. Statistics rebuild the skeleton of their story: during the time they spent at Fort Clatsop they killed 131 elk, 20 deer, otter and beaver. There were only 12 out of the 106 days spent there that they were not drenched with steady downpours of coastal rain. But, except for petty thievery, they had no trouble with their Indian neighbors.

Finally, on March 23, 1806, they began the reverse journey, arriving back in St. Louis on Tuesday, September 23, having lost only one man on the demanding journey of 28 months, who died of an incurable illness.

Today at a national memorial maintained by the United States Department of the Interior, Fort Clatsop has been reconstructed on the exact site where, a hundred years earlier, the rotting logs of the original fort were already

The replica of Fort Clatsop, whose buildings housed the 32 members of the Lewis and Clark expedition through the winter of 1805-1806, is located 4½ miles southwest of Astoria on the site of the original. The 125 acres that comprise the Fort Clatsop National Memorial also include the spring which provided the group's water supply and the landing where the boats were sheltered during the storms which assailed them through the winter. The 50-foot square stockade is centered by a small parade ground bordered by two rows of log cabins that served as living quarters and storage units. The restored site and buildings were rebuilt following the detailed drawings and instructions contained in the daily journals kept by the leaders of the "Corps of Discovery" during their voyage of exploration, one of the most important in the history of the United States.

overgrown with vines. The site's location was preserved in the memory of local residents, however, and exact replicas of the buildings were completed in 1955 as part of the Lewis and Clark Centennial Celebration.

The replica, following explicit plans drawn in the diaries, is a 50-foot square centered by a strip of parade ground which is paralleled by two rows of small log cabins with shed roofs of shingles slanting toward the center of the enclosure.

The fort's safety assured by guards having a clear view of the entire roof, the enclosure was completed by rows of logs, sharpened to points, which formed the stockade and entry gates. The men slept eight to a cabin in bunks; the Charboneaus were allotted one room, the two leaders shared a cabin, and the officers' quarters were adjacent to the storage units where their precious supplies were kept under lock and key. Each room had a rude fireplace, and they were built to ensure protection from the incessant rain.

The grounds are kept in their natural state, preserving the paths to the spring and to the canoe landing and the slough where the party's five canoes were berthed when not in use.

Supplementing the visual presentation of the actual quarters which housed the company through the winter of 1805-1806 are the exhibits and books and maps at the visitors' center, plus a half-hour film narration by TV star Lorne Green. During the summer park rangers dressed in authentic costumes enact day-to-day activities of the original party while demonstrating the frontier arts which were necessary to their survival—candle making, tanning, beadwork, making moccasins, splitting shakes, curing jerky—as part of an annual program.

Within a 25-mile radius are other historical reminders of the Lewis and Clark stay: in addition to the Salt Cairn at Seaside are Ecola State Park site near Cannon Beach where Captain Clark took Sacajawea to show her the beached whale, and the trail over Tillamook Head which leads to them. Across the river on the Washington side of the Columbia at

Fort Canby State Park is another visitors' center which presents the Lewis and Clark story.

Picnic tables are provided near the Fort Clatsop center, and overnight camping is available at Fort Stevens State Park a few miles away, providing fine camping facilities of 600 spaces, restrooms, electric stoves, fireplaces, and picnic tables all year around.

Winter or summer, a visit to Fort Clatsop Memorial offers an extraordinary opportunity to see the conditions under which the expedition survived.

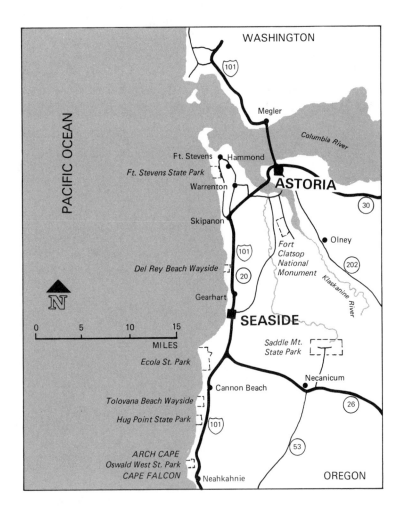

Astoria
Warrenton
Seaside
Cannon Beach

ASTORIA

Astoria is, without qualification, the historic center of Oregon. Since 1792, when Captain Robert Gray found courage to maneuver his ship, the *Columbia*, across the formidable bar and into the river that bears its name, the area has been a focal point for "firsts" in the country's history.

Following the sojourn of the Lewis and Clark "Corps of Discovery" the winter of 1805-1806, John Jacob Astor, the New York financier, organized the Pacific Fur Company in 1810 to establish an American Fur trade on the Columbia River. One half of the dual expedition brought Astor's trade ship the *Tonquin* around Cape Horn loaded with the supplies while an overland party crossed in the tracks of Lewis and Clark. The *Tonquin* party arrived six months before the land party and built Fort Astoria in 1811—the first permanent American settlement in the West.

It was a daring commercial venture but the timing was poor; the War of 1812 made the arrival of relief ships for the colony chancy. The Fort was subsequently taken by the

British and renamed Fort George. The Americans regained control in 1846 in the horsetrading that accompanied the end of the joint occupation of the Northwest by England and the United States when the boundary between the two countries was established at the 49th parallel. The Fort is now partially restored on its original site at 15th and Exchange Streets in Astoria and is open to the public.

The first post office west of the Rocky Mountains was started in 1847 by John Shively on a site near the restored Fort Astoria. A year later the first customs house on the Pacific Coast was begun when John Adair recorded the arrival of the first vessel to officially enter the Port of Astoria on April 3, 1849.

The Astoria Column

Symbol for the historical events which have centered around the city is the Astoria Column towering 125 feet atop Coxcomb Hill. Built by the Great Northern Railroad to complete a series of six historic monuments along its right of way, it was originally planned as a giant flagstaff holding an outsize American flag. However, the architect of the monument suggested a tower to be designed by Italian artist Attilio Pusterla.

The impressive tower topped by an observation balcony is finished with a series of spiral panels which depict the historic events which occurred in the region. The artist chose to finish the exterior in graffito, a form of bas-relief produced by layering white stucco over a darker concrete base and literally scratching the designs through the top layer.

It was finished in 1926 at a cost of $27,000, which was shared by the railway and a contribution from Vincent Astor, the great-grandson of the city's founder. Repaired and refinished 10 years later, the tower still requires periodic maintenance to keep deterioration to a minimum. In 1975 interior supports were constructed to slow down the cracking which has gradually worsened over the years.

The view from the top offers a spectacular vista of the Pacific beyond the mouth of the Columbia, fed by a network of rivers; several towns which have grown up along the Columbia; and, when the weather is clear, Mt. Hood and the temperamental Mt. St. Helens.

Even standing at the foot of the unique structure the view of the city and its waterfront 735 feet below is impressive. For the past few years the tower has been lighted at night, making it visible several miles out to sea.

More than 75,000 visitors a year make the trip up Coxcomb Drive to the park which surrounds the colorful monument. And nearby is another item for the city's record of "firsts"—the antenna system which carried the nation's first cable TV transmission in 1948.

The Big Fire of 1922

On December 8, 1922, the city was subjected to a traumatic series of "firsts" when, at 1:45 a.m., fire swept beneath the pilings of the waterfront business district centered along 10th Street. The business blocks, built on pilings over the river, were made with plank "basements" beneath the floors where coal for heating the establishments was stored. By the end of the second day the entire downtown business area was a mass of glowing coal fires, including a number of "red light" houses. Patients from St. Mary's Hospital were evacuated to the high school, safely out of the fire's path. The coal burned for days, business records were destroyed, and more than one merchant sent bills for amounts thought to be due, accepting customers' corrected statements as basis for payment.

Safes from many businesses fell through the burning floors into the smoldering coal piles. It was ten days before local shopowners could inspect their papers to see what had survived when they were finally opened by "professional" safebreakers.

Astoria Hotel

The pink shell of the historic Astoria Hotel stands like an aging dowager on the hillside overlooking the modernistic Maritime Museum building on the waterfront.

The elegant old building was abandoned in 1968, and the windows removed. Tentative restoration plans call for shops on the street levels, and living units on the upper floors. In the meantime, it is protected from destruction by being placed on the National Registry of Historic Places.

The Waterfront

Astoria's waterfront is the city's heartbeat. In keeping with its founding as a trade center, its development has taken place along the river which is its lifeline to sources of commerce. But fluctuating conditions in the world and advancing technology have brought changes to the dock area as old businesses have been crowded out by new ones.

Interspersed among established companies which have weathered the ups and downs of the city's fortunes are newcomers in remodeled warehouses offering services and merchandise that would have been unheard of as dock-based enterprises a few years ago.

Pier 11

Specialty shops and boutiques abound in this atrium on the docks, housed in renovated waterfront buildings between 10th and 11th streets. **The Black Murex** is a wonderland of nautical gifts and accessories for those who love the sea and its treasures. Shells, of course: baskets and bins of shells to be prized by collectors and children and those seeking souvenirs.

Linens printed with coastal motifs, soaps masquerading as starfish and sea horses, notepaper and marine prints, maps and games and kits relating to the ocean share space with a fine assortment of quality books on marine subjects. Pottery from local potters is offered at prices that seem modest considering the quality of the wares.

Nearby shops feature select assortments of gift items: unusual basketry pieces include mirrors in wicker frames; lampshades with perforated designs that show when the light shines through. An excellent assortment of greeting cards is on display. Lovely imported enamelware and gourmet kitchen utensils and fine gift food items are also to be found here.

Speciality shops and boutiques surround this atrium on the docks, a fun place to explore. Few visitors leave the complex without looking in on the unique carved sea serpent in the lounge of **The Feedstore Restaurant** on the river side of the complex. The polished hardwood hand-carved serpent supports a counter 20 feet long with its looped coils. Diners enjoy a vista of the Columbia River waterfront while lunching or dining that often includes foreign freighters at anchor just outside the window wall.

Seafood "Super" Markets

Next door to **Pier 11** is the **Ocean Foods Market** which specializes in fine foods from the sea. They aren't just kidding when they advertise *fresh fish*; visitors can watch fishing boats unloading the day's haul with a good possibility that their subsequent purchases in the sales room may include some of the same. Along with seafood still cool from the ocean deeps they also sell shrimp and crab cocktails in their own special sauce, plus smoked, kippered, pickled and canned seafood products, and sourdough bread.

Near the entrance to the Astoria toll bridge is **Josephson's Smokehouse.** Now in their 65th year in the no-nonsense box of a building with its advertising painted on the narrow siding, they merchandise the finest in Scandanavian delicacies such as sweet-and-sour pickled salmon (from an old family recipe) and their brine-cured smoked salmon. They will custom pack and ship items from their retail room to any part of the country.

Astoria Toll Bridge

This graceful bridge spans the Columbia River from the city's west end—more than four miles long, containing the world's longest truss span (1,232 feet). Completed in 1966, it was the final link in Highway 101, the transcontinental traffic route stretching from Canada to Mexico.

The Columbia River Maritime Museum

Astoria, as befits a historic city at the mouth of one of the world's great rivers, boasts the most comprehensive West Coast maritime museum north of San Francisco. The museum, since 1982, has been housed in a new building especially designed to display its treasure trove of historical exhibits in the **Maritime Park** on the waterfront at the foot of 17th Street. The courtyard is centered by the 25,000 pound anchor from the World War II battleship **Indiana**, looming like a gargantuan harpoon in front of the ultra-modern building with its upswept roofline.

Inside the rooms are filled with exhibits that chronicle 200 years of the region's marine history. A marvelous collection of ship models range in size from three inches to ten feet, including a magnificent five-masted sailing ship and a rare, large-scale model of the battleship **Oregon**, scrapped for steel during World War II.

The signal unit from the Old North Head Light Station allows visitors a close view of one of the French-made lenses that were used in signal lights built along the Pacific Coast during the 1880's. Flotsam from many north coast shipwrecks has come to rest here, including the carved name plates from the **Peter Iredale**.

The exhibits are inclusive: whaling paraphernalia, antique diving gear and marine relics share space with machinery from early-day canneries and artifacts from native cultures, to name a few. The categories seem endless and the items are fascinating. Prints of marine charts and maps are available from the museum at reasonable prices. Old books and photographs are stored here too. Star exhibit—the lightship

Columbia; retired—rides at anchor alongside the courtyard; the fourth and last **Columbia River Lightship** to serve at the mouth of the Columbia between 1892 and 1979, when an automated buoy was installed to replace her.

A magnificent model of a five-masted sailing ship, one of the outstanding collections of ships' models ranging in size from 3 inches to 10 feet.

About Town

Astoria is recognized for its outstanding examples of Victorian architecture. A single ten-block section of Franklin Avenue between 7th and 17th Streets contains more than three dozen of the grand old homes—the steep, gabled roofs and pointed arched windows of Gothic Revival sitting proudly among the flat-topped Italianate residences, and the gingerbready Queen Anne styles turreted and towered and wrapped in verandas. Another group of the elegant mansions cluster in the 1600 block on Grand Avenue.

A large number of the elegant buildings are private homes; many are churches. Most have matured with dignity and grace. Many of them are listed in the National Registry of Historic Places.

Flavel House epitomizes the Victorian houses that have become one of the landmarks of the city. Captain George Flavel, wealthy ship captain/industrialist, planned his home well in advance of the start of its construction. The foundations were laid in a block-square site already landscaped lavishly. The house was famed for the richly paneled rooms and the six ornate fireplaces, each carved to a different design from expensive woods set with imported tiles.

The house remained the residence of the Flavel family until 1933 when it was deeded to Clatsop County for use as a historical center. Since that time it has been maintained by the Clatsop County Historical Society as a museum. The drawing room now contains the fireplace from the captain's cabin of the wrecked sailing ship **Peter Iredale** whose skeleton can still be explored at Fort Stevens State Park. Outstanding marine paintings are hung throughout the building.

The house has stood the wear and tear of gales from the stormy Columbia River without noticeable damage for over a hundred years. Known far and wide as "the house with the red roof" in its early days, it served as a landmark for ships entering the Columbia estuary for many years. Now it sits, a model of quiet elegance, looking out over the harbor, no longer the center of the city's social activity, but the archivist of its past.

WARRENTON

Warrenton, the small town 15 miles around Young's Bay from Astoria is deceptive in appearance and reputation. It might seem the old fishing village, bypassed by Highway 101 as it cuts across between Astoria and Seaside, had sat out the 80 years since its incorporation without change, and planned to continue doing so in time to come.

Not so. Warrenton's development of modern boat basin facilities has initiated the transformation of the town into a prime coastal location. The moving force behind the establishment of Warrenton was Daniel Knight Warren, an entrepreneur involved in railroads, lumber mills, cattle raising, banking and logging. It was Warren who diked the Skipanon River over 100 years ago, using imported Chinese laborers to hand-work the project. From this beginning Warrenton has grown to become the charter boat center of the Columbia River.

The Skipanon River Mooring Basin, built in the mid-fifties by the US Corps of Engineers, is the focus of Warrenton's business area. Excellent charter services operate Coast Guard approved boats out of the basin for some of the finest salmon fishing in the world. Commercial seafood processors encourage visitors to come watch the canning and freezing of their product.

Artists find the picturesque town irresistable, and art galleries tucked in among tackle shops. Most buildings, if not historic, are definitely "mature." A drive through the town gives one a feeling of being transported backward in time — a rare pleasure in today's hustle-bustle world.

Young's Bay Plaza shopping center is located at the intersection of Harbor Drive and Highway 101 between Astoria and Warrenton. Small businesses cluster around a supermarket and a drugstore.

Unmarked and almost unnoticed, the wooden hulks of locally made sailing ships lie in the mud of Young's Bay, abandoned there when shipbuilding declined in the area at low tide.

Fort Stevens State Park

The star attraction of the region is **Fort Stevens**, the country's most westerly military installation from the Civil War through the end of World War II. The original earthworks, begun by Union soldiers who feared Confederate ships might come into the Columbia River, were completed the *day before* General Lee signed the surrender papers at Appomattox on April 4, 1865.

Decommissioned in 1947, after a long and honorable career, Fort Stevens was retired at the height of its fame — the only military target in the continental United States to be attacked during World War II — the first indeed since the War of 1812.

The attack came on June 22, 1942, while the country was still trying to recover from the psychological trauma of the attack on Pearl Harbor which decimated our South Pacific fleet and left our defenses vulnerable to the powerful Japanese navy. It started about 10:30 p.m. while most men at Battery Russell, the gun emplacement under attack, were asleep. The Japanese submarine *I-25* fired seventeen rounds of shells, one coming within 300 yards of the battery. Unsure of the source of the attack, officers did not order the guns fired in retaliation, although soldiers were sent to the beach in anticipation of an enemy landing craft operation.

Daily walking tours of the rusting iron installation still at Fort Stevens Military Reservation are conducted starting in June. Park rangers have been reconstructing the remaining buildings and are on hand to answer questions.

Also within the Fort Stevens State Park is the wreckage of the **Peter Iredale**, a British ship grounded in 1907 during a storm while on its way from Australia to Portland to take on a load of wheat. The skeleton of the 287-foot four-masted sailing ship, driven into the "shelving sands" by a strong current, remains there, slowly disintegrating, too deeply imbedded to be moved.

The End Of The Jetty

A good road through Fort Stevens State Park leads to an observation platform, on the dunes at the end of the south jetty, which overlooks the mouth of the Columbia River from the Oregon side. Ocean winds attack fiercely from the river's entrance, hard enough to sway the heavy timbered structure. The great chunks of black rock that make up the barrier jetty are paralleled by a decaying wooden trestle barely wide enough to accommodate a set of rusty railroad tracks, relics of the narrow-gauge rail line that carried the monstrous boulders from the quarry workers during the jetty's construction. Crashing breakers underscore the dangers mariners face in crossing the treacherous Columbia River Bar, known to the world's mariners for centuries as The Graveyard of the Pacific because of the number of vessels wrecked there.

Annual Events

Great Astoria Crab Feed—dinner, craft and food booths, beer garden, boat tours, exhibits in March.

Scandinavian Midsummer Festival—a weekend celebration of the area's ethnic heritage in mid-June.

The Astoria Regatta—a maritime celebration with land parade, water events, beer garden, craft and food booths, Queen's ball—mid-August.

Great Columbia Crossing—8½ mile marathon across the Astoria bridge, October.

Two fine swimming areas at Coffenbury Lake in Fort Stevens State Park are equipped with bath houses and log booms for the convenience of those enjoying its sandy beaches. A boat launching ramp at the north end is an added attraction for enthusiasts who come for the excellent trout and perch fishing. A 2½-mile hiking trail encircles the lake itself, and more trails wind through the park. A large picnic area borders the lake, and facilities at the adjacent campground include 225 trailer sites with utility hookups, 120 improved campsites, and 260 tent sites.

SEASIDE

Seaside is a coastal resort town — Oregon's largest — designed for that role by its founder, transportation king Ben Holladay, who covered the West with railroads and stage coaches, and established shipping routes to supplement them.

In 1871 Holladay built a lavish seaside hotel in the area first settled by a Scot, Alexander Latty, a ship's captain with the Hudson Bay Company, and Solomon Smith, a teacher at Fort Vancouver. Attractive extras for the recreation-minded patron of *Seaside House* included a race track and the horses to run, and a wild animal zoo. These, plus the beauty of the golden beach, insured its immediate popularity. The colorful Holladay, as much a showman as P.T. Barnum, required his fleet of coastal steamers to salute the flag which flew from the Seaside House's rooftop flagstaff with cannon fire each time they passed.

Replacements of the old boardwalk along Seaside's ocean front in the early 1920's established the city once and for all as an ocean resort in the grand manner, and it became known as the Coastal Capital of Oregon. Today the fine old hotels and residences fronted by the Prom are being elbowed aside by modern resorts whose glittering glass and steel tend to overpower the fading glory of the genteel originals.

A must stop is **Fenton's Farmers Market** on Highway 101 north of Seaside, a thriving market/garden shop for almost 20 years. The market section in the older building is fronted by buckets of cut flowers whose colors glow on the rainiest days. Top quality fruits and vegetables add their own bold colors: as bright as illustrations in a deluxe seed catalog. Wooden crates serve as bins for produce from which customers can pick and choose produce piece by piece.

It's strictly a self-serve establishment. Brown eggs are one of the most popular items. Oregon honey is dispensed from a large container near the counter built from 18-inch-square driftwood timbers from an old shipwreck. Gift items and Oregon crafts are displayed along with the food products.

The garden shop was designed and built by an English architect, a tourist who visited the market in its early days and became a friend of the owners. Plank walls in design patterns are hung with pages from old newspapers displayed behind glass panels. Ceiling rafters form a rectangular lattice effect beneath translucent roof panels. The building is heated by large iron drum-type stoves, fired by wood cut and split by the owners.

The garden showroom is flanked on both sides by outdoor patio areas in which nursery plants and trees are displayed as part of the landscaping. From this point, inside or out, one views charming vistas of plants, hangings, and wall sections. The front patio roof is supported by a row of cedar telephone poles.

The week before Memorial Day each year, a huge central room behind the main market section is banked ceiling high on all four walls with cannisters of fresh flowers. People come from all over the Northwest coast to select floral tributes from among the quality flowers on display.

Some Special Shops

Special shops line the streets: gift, antique, jewelry, book, sports, candy and fashion shops to delight holiday browsers. You pay your money and take your choice in Seaside.

But no trip to Seaside is complete without a visit to **Harrison's Bakery** on Broadway close downtown. Founded in 1914, the bakery produces hundreds of loaves of special recipe breads a day in addition to scrumptious cookies, pastries, and such. All are made from scratch, using natural ingredients and no preservatives. Harrison's baked goods taste the way we all remember "homemade."

As would be expected there are eateries to suit every taste and purse, from fine dinner houses that include the long-time favorite **Crab Broiler** to restaurants for casual dining — **Kan's Hankow Inn** (serving Chinese food for almost fifty years at the same location, and **Norma's** noted for seafood, both on Broadway — and a full compliment of fast food and deli spots.

The **Seaside Aquarium** is nearing the half-century mark. Located two blocks north of the Turnaround on the Prom, it is noted for its harbor seals. "Youngsters" from one to ninety-nine are entranced by their amusing performances. The outstanding assortment of marine life exhibits — up to 1500 varieties — includes sharks and an octopus.

A few blocks south of The Turnaround, just below the Prom in a small courtyard boxed in by residences, is the replica of the **Lewis and Clark Salt Cairn**, where a small detachment of men from the historic expedition spent the better part of two months making salt the winter of 1806.

The low rock cairn is constructed to specifications found in the expedition diaries and mounds to a flattened top to hold small "kittles" like the ones in which three to four quarts of salt were produced daily while the project was in operation.

Ultimately four bushels were obtained which provided a "most agreeable addition" to the limited diets of the men at Fort Clatsop fourteen miles to the north. The twelve gallons packed in small kegs and laid by for the return voyage proved valuable as trade goods as well as for personal use on game, roots, fish, and roast dog which made up the menu during the trip home.

The cairn has been reconstructed on the exact site of the original, established through the memory of Jenny Mishel, a woman of the Clatsop tribe whose father had shown her the spot when she was a child.

The monument, maintained in its natural state as nearly as fences, plaques, and walkways will allow, helps to illuminate a minor facet of one of the most significant voyages of exploration in the history of the United States.

Raintree Gift and Garden Center at the southern end of Seaside on Highway 101 was originally conceived as a gift shop that would carry a few houseplants. The first year the plants proved to be the main attraction, and the **Raintree** now specializes in unusual and hard to find plantings. Available here are such items as orange and lemon trees, lilacs, and a variety of succulents.

A well-stocked service area holds almost any tool or supply gardeners need. Clients come from all over the country, with a sprinkling of foreign visitors. One devoted patron voiced the sentiments of their many repeat customers when she remarked, "I wouldn't dream of leaving Seaside without stopping at the Raintree."

Annual Events

Major events are scheduled the year around at Seaside. Many of them begin and/or end at **The Turnaround** — the official end point of the Lewis and Clark Trail. The landmark seems diminished by the crowded street leading to it and the limited parking. But it's there, and just beyond is the beautiful stretch of sandy beach which has been one of Seaside's main attractions since the original rocky beach was covered with sand in the early part of the century.

The **Trail's End Marathon**, held each year in February, has grown a thousandfold in the 15 years of its existence. Organized to draw tourists to the resort town during the off-season, it has succeeded far beyond the goals of the contest's developers. The race begins on the beach near the Turnaround when hundreds of entrants — kindergarteners to senior citizens — gather for the start of the 26-mile endurance contest. Only about three-fourths of the contestants finish the race, but all entrants receive a Trail's End T-shirt. Nearly as many spectators line the course to cheer the runners on as enter the race.

An outstanding fireworks display is presented from the beach at the Turnaround on the Fourth of July each year; and the Christmas Season is officially opened with a beach lighting ceremony during Thanksgiving weekend.

The modern convention center which can accommodate groups of 2000 is also the scene for traditional events. **The Great Pumpkin Community Halloween Party** is held each October 31.

In mid-July emphasis is on quality rather than quantity as the **Miss Oregon Pageant**, state finals for the Miss America Pageant in Atlantic City, are held. The spotlight is turned on Oregon's loveliest young women as they vie for the opportunity to represent the state in the national contest.

Each year Seaside becomes more what it was designed to be: one of the most attractive resort towns on the Northwest coast.

Notes:

The Seaside Turnaround at the end of Broadway is a traditional gathering place. Viewed from the balcony of the Seasider Hotel, it looks much the same as it did in the days of excursion trains and early motor cars.

CANNON BEACH

The rusty cannon for which Cannon Beach was named, mounted near the north end of the loop road that leads from Highway 101 to the resort village, was washed ashore from the wreckage of the schooner *Shark* in 1846. But that martial artifact is out of tone with the creative energy that sparks the town's activities.

For **Cannon Beach** is a center for artists — painters, sculptors, weavers, metalsmiths, photographers; artisans in stained glass, calligraphy, needlework — and the galleries and shops where their work is displayed. Resort towns reflect the tone of the shops that represent a major attraction for the tourists and vacationers on which the communities thrive. The emphasis in Cannon Beach is on quality. Business names help generate an innovative atmosphere that supports creativity: **Thistledown Gift Shop** (chimes and porcelain and jewelry and carvings); **Fair Winds** (scrimshaw and brass and ship's clocks and quality nautical artifacts); **Once Upon a Breeze** (kites); **The Sandpiper Gallery** (presenting works of regional artists in assigned-time showings); **'Tis The Season** (a year around Christmas shop with all the trimmings, plus consulting services); **Geppetto's Toy Shoppe** (imported toys).

Specialty shops stand shoulder to shoulder along Hemlock Street; notably, **Bruce's Candy Kitchen**, the granddaddy of them all, with glass counters filled with tempting trays of homemade chocolates, bins of salt water taffy, and other delicious sweets; topped by big glass jars of licorice whips and jelly beans and such long-time favorites.

Not easily passed by is **The Ice Creamery**. The small shop reflects proprietor Jim Osburn's personal taste in art. The walls behind the ice cream case are hung with his private collection of the works of local artists. The ice cream counter is set up behind two decorative carved wooden pillars, part of the original old store building, now painted gold. Ice cream is from the Alpenrose Dairies near Portland — 24 flavors.

Will and Judy Osburn operate the grocery and delicatessen next door — **The Gourmet Food Store for Thrifty**

Gourmets — which sells custom made sandwiches and homemade take-outs. These are fun places to shop. Try them!

The round building across the street from Bruce's Candy Kitchen houses **Pat's Baskets and Coffees**. The shop carries an exceptional assortment of woven containers, from party cups to outsized hampers and trays; plus one of the largest collections of wall baskets in the Northwest. The coffee section is stocked with fine blends and brands of coffee and tea, and displays of quality gift servers and accessories, including espresso and cappuccino makers. The owner also serves coffee and tea by the cup and provides small tables for customers while they enjoy them.

Ecola State Park adjacent to Cannon Beach is known for the spectacular coastal scenery within its borders. Plentiful picnic sites (with camp stoves) are available for those wishing to take advantage of the excellent swimming, hiking, fishing, and beachcombing. It was to this area that Captain Lewis brought Sacajawea to show her the beached whale during the winter the expedition spent at Fort Clatsop.

The complex of red buildings with the white gingerbread trim as travelers come into Cannon Beach from the north looks like a setting from a Walt Disney movie — but they aren't. This is **Cannon Beach Conference Center**, a non-denominational Christian center that offers non-credit Bible classes through the school year; with lectures, workshops, and retreats held in summer. The modern facility can house 300 guests and feed 400, and includes a snack bar, a bakery and a bookstore along with motel units and dining room. Motels and resorts serve the area, from "older and smaller" to "large and luxurious." **Sea Ranch Trailer Village** at the north end of town provides RV accommodations.

Restaurants in like number and similar category range offer good eating, from the hanburger/hot dog/homemade chili menu at **Bill's Tavern** to the family atmosphere at **Morrison's Fireside Restaurant** in the log house and the elegant dining at **Daggatts** at Tolovana.

Famed **Haystack Rock**, the world's third largest coastal monolith, is the landmark which centers the nine-mile long beach fronting this cluster of shops, restaurants, and natural recreational accommodations for vacationers and tourists. Created over the ages by pounding tides which shaped it from mountains long since turned to sand, the 235-foot rock is still undergoing change. Since the turn of the century two of its small side "needles" have been devoured by the sea, leaving two to go.

The tidepools at the base of the rock become a living museum at low tide, with ever-changing exhibits of crabs, mussels, starfish, and anemones. The rock itself is a national bird sanctuary offering visitors opportunities to observe the marine fowl which live there.

The rock was lighted at night during a short period several years ago, but environmentalists forced the removal of the floodlights, believing they would disturb the wildlife.

Tide pools at the base of Haystack Rock (Cannon Beach) hold a fascinating group of intertidal animals. This is a protected area, however, so living creatures may not be taken there.

Haystack Summer Workshop is a summer-long program of quality seminars and workshops, keyed to the arts and the environment, presented annually through **Portland State University**. Led by gifted and recognized instructors in music, art, photography, fine crafts and creative writing areas, the program is designed to coordinate with family vacations. A full program is offered for children 4-13 years of age, including beachcombing, hiking, field trips as well as theatre, music and art. The structured courses are planned on a credit/non-credit basis to suit individual preferences. Workshop information can be obtained from Portland State University, 1-800-452-4909 (Oregon) or 1-800-547-8887 out-of-state.

The **Coaster Theater** is a year around operation, featuring drama, comedy, musical and music performances, and dance. Summer season, traditionally presented by Portland State University Players, is now being presented by resident Repertory Company. Guest artists appear frequently. This is intimate theatre at its best, well adapted to the small (200 seat) facility. And prices are affordable.

Annual Events

Cannon Beach retains its atmosphere of small-town charm that holds through the onslaught of hundreds of contestants plus thousands of spectators who show up every year for the **Cannon Beach Sandcastle Contest**, held each year between late June and mid-July. What began as a children's activity about 20 years ago now includes adults — limited to 100 teams — and prizes awarded in a number of special categories. The contest starts in the morning, with contestants allowed about three hours in which to create their masterpieces; spectators have time for viewing and snapping photographs between the start of judging and the time when the tides sweep them away in a spectacular finale.

Kite Flying Contest — Second weekend after Labor Day in September.

Community Christmas Play — Coaster Theatre, first two weekends in December.

Notes:

The Cape Meares Lighthouse just south of Tillamook Bay along the Netarts-Oceanside loop, is one of the most picturesque of the Oregon coast. When built in 1890, it was intended for the point that is presently called Cape Lookout. Due to a survey mixup which switched the names, the lighthouse was built on the former Cape Lookout, published on maps as Cape Meares (which it has remained). Now unmanned, it remains a favorite of visitors.

The Lighthouses

Oregon's six lighthouses seem fragile, toylike, to be standing guard along a primitive coastline carved by an ocean reaching halfway around the globe. But titanic waves generated by 6,000 miles of empty seas, colliding with the continent's edge in continuous assault, make them necessary. A shoreline sculpted from prehistoric mountains made construction of these isolated towers, built during the last half of the 19th century, as dangerous as navigation of the treacherous off-shore waters which imperiled Captain Cook's ship *Resolution* during his exploration of the Pacific coast one hundred years earlier.

The first lighthouse on the 350-mile long coast, the **Umpqua River Light Station** 20 miles north of Coos Bay, was built in 1857, but within four years it had fallen into the sea, undermined by erosion of the dunes on which it was built. For the next nine years ships in adjacent coastal waters reverted to navigation by visual landmarks such as the white shell mounds accumulated during Indian ceremonies over the years which were visible at great distances from the sea.

In 1866 **Cape Gregory Lighthouse** was erected near the entrance to Coos Bay, but the eight-sided building with a frame of wrought iron had to be moved within a few years because the sea, eating into the connecting rock, had formed a channel between the lighthouse and the mainland. It was replaced by a second tower closer to the shore, which ultimately had to be moved for the same reason as its predecessor.

The present facility was renamed **Cape Arago Lighthouse** after the headland several miles to the south. It is still

37

separated by a sea channel, tied now to the mainland by a footbridge built after the basket on a cable, which ferried early light keepers and supplies to their station, dumped one man onto the rock below. The station's 110,000 candlepower light is identified by a distinctive relay of three flashes at 20-second intervals. The lighthouse is located on Coast Guard property, and personnel residing there maintain the light, fog signal, and radio beacon which make up the light station.

In 1868 the original **Yaquina Head Light Station** was raised on the north side of the Yaquina Bay entrance. Replaced six years later at another site, the first building is now maintained as a historic exhibit by the Oregon State Parks system. It is open to the public from mid-May to Labor Day, furnished in the style of its origin. Local legend has inhabited the old tower with the ghost of a former keeper's wife who is said to walk the empty halls now and then. The tower itself is indicated as a day mark on current marine charts.

Two years later a lighthouse was built on Cape Blanco, originally Cape Orford. Heavy trees were cleared from the face of the Cape to make a place for the 59-foot white tower and separate keeper's house nearby. Bricks for the buildings were manufactured in the area from local clay. The white light of the **Cape Blanco Lighthouse** is projected through a Fresnel system French lens which transforms a 1,000 watt lightbulb into a distinctive pattern of flashes which skippers can identify more than 20 miles out to sea. The mechanical light replaces burned out bulbs automatically, assuring continuous production of the 300,000 candlepower beam. At 250 feet above sea level, Cape Blanco's light is Oregon's highest as well as the farthest south and west. With resident keepers, it is the only Oregon light station which maintains regular, although limited, visiting hours.

The present **Yaquina Head Light Station** was built four miles north of the entrance to Yaquina Bay on 1,935 acres of reserve land authorized in 1866 by President Andrew Johnson. Supplies for construction of the 96-foot cone-shaped tower were hoisted up the cliff face by windlass. The building was completed in August of 1873—but at the wrong site! The station had been designated for Otter Crest, several miles to the north. Automated in 1966, the 110,000 candle-power light projects through the original lens manufactured in Paris in 1868. The signal, a sequence of two white flashes every 20 seconds, shows 162 feet above the water for a range of 50 miles. The station is open for inspection on special occasions only.

The installation of **Tillamook Rock Light**, begun in 1879 on a massive rock a mile offshore and 20 miles south of the mouth of the Columbia River, has the most dramatic history of Oregon's light stations. The exposed site, barely 200 feet above tideline, could serve as a substitute location for "The Exorcist."

The construction crew and materials were transported to the dangerous setting by breeches buoy, and the top of the rock was leveled by blasting crews before work could start on the stone building. Basalt rocks shaped to precision fit at an inland quarry were shipped to the rock by lighthouse tender. The workmen labored under impossible conditions, persistently threatened by heavy seas pounding over the site.

The light station was completed in 1881, after 18 months of arduous labor (including six months' delay due to storm damage which partially destroyed the project) at a cost of one life and $125,000. But the troubles were just beginning. Keepers were at the mercy of a merciless ocean which often sent boulders crashing through walls and into the light itself.

Ships trying to enter the Columbia River were depen-dent upon the Tillamook Rock Light, the only navigational signal south of Cape Disappointment, for a safe entry into the river's mouth. The 76-year-old light was maintained at a pro-hibitive cost until September of 1957, when it was replaced by an automated signal and the original installations were abandoned.

It has subsequently passed through the hands of a series of private buyers. NO TRESPASSING signs keep visitors from landing at the rock, but it is visible from Tillamook Head—a disintegrating monument to the men who challenged the destructive power of the Pacific Ocean to install the beacon.

In 1890 the small **Cape Meares Lighthouse** was established near Tillamook Bay. Authorized for construction on Cape Lookout 10 miles farther south, the materials were delivered to the wrong site in the roadless wilderness. The installation was subsequently legalized by a special congressional bill during the term of President Benjamin Harrison. The manned lighthouse was replaced by an automated station in 1963—a 17-foot facility 232 feet atop the Cape,

A familiar sight on Oregon beaches is a lonely lighthouse materializing against the shoreline as early morning mists are chased away by the sun.

In 1894, some 33 years after the first lighthouse on the Umpqua River fell into the sea, the second **Umpqua River Lighthouse** was built on a safer, higher spot at the same location. The white tower 165 feet above sea level houses the only red/white flashing signal on the Oregon coast. With candlepower of 400,000 for the white light and 200,000 for the red, the signal alternates two white flashes with one red flash every 15 seconds. The light station is operated by the Umpqua River Lifeboat Station.

Also in 1894, the **Heceta Head Lighthouse** was built on the coast between Florence and Yachats, 28 miles north of the first station on the Umpqua. Materials for the 56-foot tower were shipped from San Francisco, then hauled in wagons along the beach and over the mountain to the setting. The light stands 205 feet high on the rocky headland, its 1,500,000 candlepower beam flashing a steady white light. The station is manned by resident light keepers.

Although only Cape Blanco Lighthouse maintains visiting hours as such, it is sometimes possible to obtain permission to visit light stations by contacting the Coast Guard units at Cape Arago, Yaquina Head, and on the Umpqua River. And whether inspected close up or from vantage points along the coast, there is an atmosphere of romance and adventure about the sturdy outpost towers scattered along the rocky coastline which seems to linger from another era that has all but disappeared from our lives today.

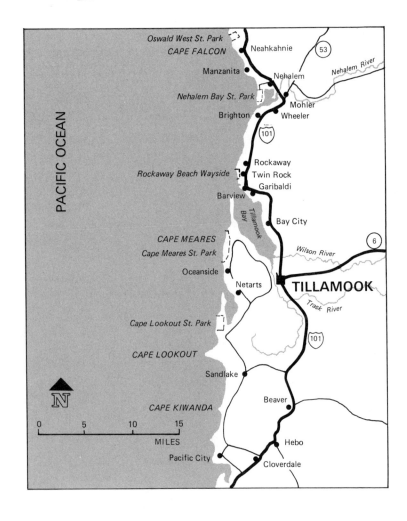

Oswald West St. Park
CAPE FALCON
Neahkahnie
53
Nehalem River
Manzanita
Nehalem
Nehalem Bay St. Park
Mohler
Wheeler
Brighton
101
PACIFIC OCEAN
Rockaway
Rockaway Beach Wayside
Twin Rock
Garibaldi
Barview
Tillamook Bay
Bay City
CAPE MEARES
Wilson River
6
Cape Meares St. Park
Oceanside
Netarts
TILLAMOOK
Trask River
Cape Lookout St. Park
101
CAPE LOOKOUT
Sandlake
N
Beaver
CAPE KIWANDA
0   5   10   15
MILES
Hebo
Pacific City
Cloverdale

Tillamook
Nehalem

TILLAMOOK COUNTY

The Tillamook County beach area is for those who want to enjoy coastal adventure without crowds. At Manzanita Junction Highway 101 makes a turn inland, to begin a 40-odd mile drive that loops around **Nehalem and Tillamook Bays**, and includes some of the most delightful recreational areas on the north coast. Some three dozen parks — State, County Federal (Forest Service, BLM) are maintained for public use in the area, supplemented by several that are operated by individuals.

Nehalem Bay is fed by a single river, the Nehalem, which drains a section of land reaching two-thirds of the way to Portland, beginning just 12 miles from the Columbia River. The Nehalem estuary is narrow, and outlets to the south near the Tillamook mouth. This is an area filled with history and legend. Predominant is the legend of Neahkahnie Mountain, and it is true that a mysterious English vessel came to rest in the bay some time around the 1790's. Lesser treasures — old bottles and relics from ships — are still found by scuba divers working several areas of Nehalem Bay.

Nehalem at the north end of the drive is a novelist's image of a bayside village come to life. There is a dreamlike quality to the small town overlooking its tranquil bay, as an old women sits in her rocking chair on a homestead porch recalling the impatient yearnings of youth while relishing the comforts achieved through the compromises demanded by age.

And there is much tangible evidence of past dreams in Nehalem, the "antique center of the Oregon coast." Every other shop seems to offer pretested merchandise to tempt those who love heritage furnishings and glass and china and— you name it. It's here in Nehalem. Many sell antiques *plus*, and most are located within shouting distance of each other in the "center" of town where the highway scoots down the hill and makes an abrupt turn. Along with vintage treasures can be found works of modern artisans who are creating tomorrow's heirlooms.

Free boat launchings and private moorings are a convenience for fishers and boaters who favor the quiet river bay over more crowded sites. Most travelers will leave Nehalem's serene setting with regret.

Although access for fishing and clamming is available all around **Tillamook Bay** most of the action takes place at the boat basin at **Garibaldi** on the northern edge of the estuary. Launching and mooring facilities for private boats, and restaurants with good food are located at the boat basin. Scuba divers enjoy spearfishing around nearby rocks and on the north jetty of the bay entrance.

Sightseeing is best on the bay's south side toward Cape Meares. There the ocean has made inroads into the land, leaving huge gray tree trunks and gnarled roots upon the beach. Stretching northward from this eroded area is the narrow peninsula that separates Tillamook Bay from the Pacific. At one time it held the community of Bayocean, developed as a lavish resort, which has since fallen into the ocean, its foundations eaten away by the tides.

The town of **Tillamook** is the county seat and largest community of the area. Located away from the ocean on the inland side of the bay, it is the locale of the world-famed Tillamook County Cheese Factory. In pioneer days it was isolated from the rest of the territory and seldom visited by traders. Settlers there built their own schooner in 1854, naming it the *Morning Star*.

Also here is the **Tillamook County Pioneer Museum** housed in an imposing stone building built in 1905 to replace the original county courthouse that burned two years earlier. Its three floors of exhibits contain replicas of a pioneer home and of the stump house which housed the area's original settler; Indian artifacts and photographs; mineral, rock and fossil collections, plus an extensive wildlife collection (over 500 specimens). A vehicle exhibit features the last stagecoach to make the mail run between Tillamook and Yamhill along with antique cars. The Museum also maintains a research library and photograph collection.

The Museum is easy to spot in downtown Tillamook at 2106 Second Street. It is open from 8:30 am-5:00 pm weekdays; noon to 5:00 pm Sundays; and closed Mondays between October 1 and May 1. A modest admission fee is offset by guest parking permits, and well worth the price.

To the west of Tillamook are the small communities of **Netarts** and **Oceanside**. Netarts is situated on Netarts Bay — a closed estuary (no river flows into it) and thus having a high salinity. Clams, crabs and bottom fish are abundant. The sandy peninsula that extends between the bay and the Pacific Ocean holds a fascinating archaeological site. It is a location of the deserted Indian village. It also offers miles of uninterrupted beachcombing.

Oceanside boasts a dandy beach that erodes each winter to a gravelly layer that contains a wealth of agates. The picturesque pedestrian tunnel hewn through the rock point at the north end of Oceanside is sometimes plagued by slides, with access to the seashells and jade-like green rocks on the other beach beyond limited to low tide.

Pacific City, south of the town of Tillamook, is small, with limited tourist facilities. But it is home to the Dory fishermen who gather to launch through the milder surf in the shelter of Cape Kiwanda. Fishing charters are available from the local dorymen. The return trip provides a thrilling ride through the breakers to a skidding stop on the sandy beach.

Scuba divers can find scallops and ling cod on the offshore reefs and pinnacles that reach to within 30 feet of the ocean's surface. Waters are usually clear, and scallops are abundant if divers can spot them in their seaweed camouflage. This sport offers a combination of adventures — undersea sport and boating through the surf!

Spectators enjoy the excitement at a distance as the dories come and go through the breakers; or by watching the hanggliders sail their colorful crafts from the heights of the cape. Pacific City offers excitement for those who seek it and peace for those who wish to stroll the uncrowded beach along the sandspit that separates the Nestucca River from the sea — five miles of beach between Cape Kiwanda and the river's mouth, much of it underdeveloped.

James Seeley White
Seashells of the Pacific Northwest
Diving for Northwest Relics
The Hedden Store Handbook
The Spells of Lamazee

Rebuilt stores like the Nehalem Bay Trading Company offer excellent shopping for gifts, antiques, and nautical relics in the town of Nehalem. A piano player entertains visitors during the arts festival.

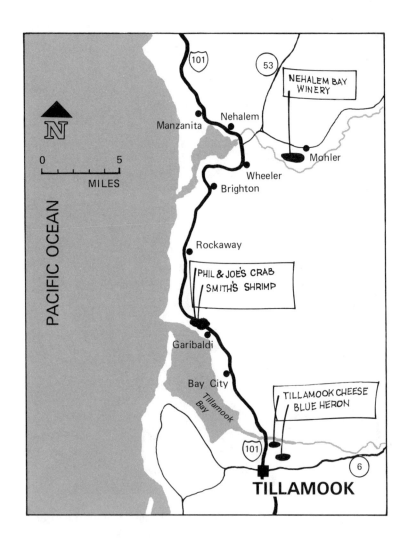

The Tillamook County Cheese Food and Wine Tour

The northern anchor for the tour is **Nehalem Bay Winery** located on Mohler Road south and west from Nehalem. Owners Pat and Adrienne McCoy produce grape varietals and house blends, plus fruit and berry wines made from premium northwest products. Visitors including tour groups are encouraged to browse through the attractive winery housed in a converted cheese factory sampling the wines in the handsome tasting room with its driftwood bar and to enjoy the art gallery upstairs. The winery is open seven days a week 10:00 in the morning until 5:00 in the evening. Nehalem Bay tasting rooms are located at Seaside on Highway 101, and at **Ecola Village** at Cannon Beach, open 11:00 am to 6:00 pm.

Karla's Crabs on Highway 101 at **Rockaway** is open daily from mid-March through October stocking seafood "as you like it" — fresh, frozen or smoked — 10:00 am to 7:00 pm.

At **Garibaldi**, midway on the tour, a jackpot of seafood plants awaits tourists. **Phil & Joe's Crab Company**, open every day 9:00 am to 6:00 pm (later hours in summer) is easy to spot on Highway 101 coming into town. Branches are also located in Tillamook and Manzanita.

Smith's Pacific Shrimp Company on the wharf has a large viewing room where visitors can observe the processing of their wares; their sales room is open April through October, 9:00 am to 5:00 pm.

Bay Front Bakery on Highway 101 in Garibaldi adds fresh bread and pastries to the variety of products offered by participating businesses of the wine-tour group. It opens at 7:00 am daily except Tuesdays.

Tillamook Cheese Factory, the largest cheese processing plant in the world, is open daily, 9:00 am to 5:00 pm. Famed internationally for its Tillamook cheddar cheese, the plant has a glass-walled viewing room where visitors who come to the plant (more than half a million a year) may observe the various steps in cheese making along with a slide/tape presentation of supplemental information on Tillamook dairy products. The dairy bar and tasting room, featuring the company's superlative ice cream as well as cheese, is also open daily, and sales personnel will wrap and mail gift packs on request. The factory is easily located from the highway by the near-life-sized, seaworthy replica of the pioneer schooner *Morning Star* in the courtyard fronting the building.

The **Blue Heron French Cheese Factory** on Blue Heron Drive at the south end of Tillamook opens its tasting room daily for sampling and sales of the French-style cheeses that are their specialty — Brie and a soft breakfast cheese — plus imported cheeses. The retail room also carries imported coffees, specialty foods and gift items. One corner is countered off as a tasting room featuring Knudsen-Erath wines. They are open from 8:00 am to 5:00 pm, with later summer hours.

The **Old Trapper Sausage Factory** in the same complex features smoked meats, sausage and jerky; open 9:00 am to 6:00 pm summers, with shorter winter hours.

The Cheese Food & Wine Tasting Tour offers an excellent opportunity for tourists to sample Oregon products which have gained well-deserved reputations for quality. It's a do-it-yourself project that's hard to beat.

The **Morning Star II** is a full-scale replica of the schooner built in 1854 by settlers of the isolated Tillamook Bay area to provide a means of marketing their products, since they were usually by-passed by coastal traders. It is on display near the entrance to the Tillamook Cheese Factory, whose quality products are shipped throughout the world.

Before leaving Tillamook take time to visit the veteran **Victory House** restaurant in the city's center. House specialties are homemade bread fresh from the oven, served with homemade wild blackberry jam.

Annual Events

Blessing of the Fleet at Garibaldi in March.
Mid-winter Swiss Festival Tillamook, also in March.
Nehalem Bay Canoe Races in May.
Art Festival, Nehalem, in July.
Tillamook County Fair at the Fairgrounds in Tillamook, August.

Pacific City is home of the adventurous dory fleet. Dr. James McMillan, owner of **Salty**, is an ardent scuba diver as well as fisherman. When the swells run three feet or less in height, as on this day, the sea is quiet enough to dive on the off-shore reef.

A display of glass floats entered in competition at the annual
Beachcombers Fair, usually held on Memorial Day weekend at
Netarts.

Notes:

The Whales

The whale, whose species have produced the most massive creatures ever to inhabit our planet, is having difficulty staying alive in a shrinking world. Technology which has, in effect, reduced the earth to a 24-hour circumference has also escalated threats to these peaceful mammals, as it has to all marine life.

Herds of blue whales—animals large enough for Jonah to have swum through their heart valves—have been reduced to an estimated 6 percent of their original population. Gray whales which once thrived in the world's oceans numbered only a few thousand by the 1930's. The Atlantic gray whales are no more. Only a group of California grays, protected by international treaty for the last 40 years, hold their own.

The semi-annual 8,000-mile journey by the grays from breeding grounds in Baja California to summer feeding grounds in the Bering Sea and back again—the longest migra-

A carved memorial panel (left) beside the parking area at the end of the South Jetty Road (Florence) commemorates the 41 sperm whales which beached themselves and died there June 16, 1979. Best time for whale watching on the Oregon coast is December through April in early morning. These mighty giants have roamed the world's oceans for over 50 million years. They are the deepest divers of any animal, communicate by voice over vast distances, and have the largest brains of any animal on earth. Carver George von der Linden contributed the carving on the marker placed by the Eugene Greenpeace Foundation.

tion of any animal—offers Oregonians a ringside seat to observe them often during the year.

The trip south begins in early fall and brings them close in to the Oregon shore. The most visible sign of their presence will be blow spouts—small feathery umbrellas of water against the sky—as they pass. If viewers are lucky, the whales may be seen breaching also, leaping from the water to silhouette briefly against the horizon in arcs which seem amazingly graceful, considering their bulk. Gray whales grow to lengths of 35-50 feet. The infants are 14-17 feet long and average 1,500 pounds at birth.

Sperm whales, deep-water feeders, are not so easily spotted during migration. When they do come in to shore, it is usually a matter of life and death, literally. Prime example is the beaching of 41 sperm whales near Florence the evening of June 16, 1979. By the time scientists and environmentalists reached the stranded whales, internal damage caused by their massive weight, minus suspension in water, made death inevitable.

A memorial marker in the parking area at the north end of the South Jetty Road in Florence commemorates this mass suicide of the creatures. Created by George von der Linden, the 6 foot-square carving of weathered cedar carries a simple statement describing the incident and the reminder that man shares the planet with other species, and all are depending on an interacting environment.

Best time for whale watching on the Oregon coast is December through April, in early morning. But they can be spotted any time from the headlands and viewpoints along the shore.

Cape Perpetua, the Oregon coast's highest promontory, which rises 800 feet above the ocean, offers excellent viewpoints for watching the gray whales as they make their annual 8,000-mile journey south each fall from the Bering Sea to Baja California. A side road leads to this viewpoint off U.S. 101 south of Waldport.

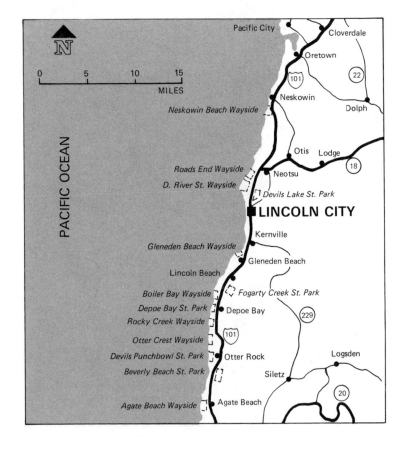

Lincoln City
Depoe Bay

LINCOLN CITY

Lincoln City is an amalgamation of small communities that includes Nelscott, Taft, Oceanlake, DeLake, and Cutler City which incorporated in 1965 to develop the area as a tourist center. The year-around population of 5,000 often swells to five times that number during the height of the summer vacation season. Lincoln City, at the top end of the Oregon coast's "Twenty Miracle Miles," offers every possible convenience and accommodation for travelers and vacationers, from campgrounds and RV parks to luxury motels that rank with the country's best; plus restaurants in a price scale that extends from the least expensive of the fast-food chains through to the finest of gourmet cuisine.

Recreational facilities abound. Along with natural beaches and lakes and streams — some of the loveliest in the world — are to be found superior shops, excellent golf courses, and superior galleries where the works of members of the growing fine arts community are displayed. Water sports are prominent among area activities.

To the south of the city is the **D River**, a narrow stretch of water 440 feet long that winds between shores strewn with driftwood from Devil's Lake on its short trip to the Pacific. Signs at north and south ends of the bridge across the little stream proclaim it the "world's shortest river." And so it is. In 1940 the US Geodetic-Geographic Board certified it as such, after determining its accurate length at low tide. And in 1973 the "Guiness Book of World Records" listed the D as the world's shortest, along with the Nile as the world's longest river.

Devil's Lake, the long curved body of water that feeds the tiny river, is Lincoln City's popular spot for water skiing and sailing, with trout fishing open year-round as well. But the real excitement comes in mid-September when boaters from all over the country join the annual hydroplane races. For two days, one-at-a-time racers skim across the water, often setting new world records. One enthusiast calls it "the Bonneville Salt Flats of sea racing." Indian legend has kept alive tales of a resident sea monster akin to Scotland's Loch Ness creature and British Columbia's Ogopogo who inhabits Lake Okanogan, but without their record of recorded sightings.

A public boat ramp, picnic tables, playground equipment, and restrooms are in Regatta Grounds Park on the lake. Similar facilities are found in the park area at the end of Holmes Road. Over one hundred camping and trailer sites are available.

Kirtsis Park in the center of Lincoln City is home for a bronze statue of Abraham Lincoln, the work of Washington, D.C., sculptress Anne Hyatt Huntington. The statue was given to Lincoln City when the city incorporated in 1965 by Governor Mark Hatfield, who felt it was the most fitting site for the statue presented as a gift to the people of Oregon by the artist.

Points of Interest

For 35 years **Lacey's Doll and Antique Museum** has been a landmark in the Lincoln City area. The Lacey collection of over 4000 dolls has been displayed at this same location on Highway 101 for over three decades. More than 10,000 visitors a year come to view the cases of dolls in the long showroom, many of them from other countries.

Most of the dolls — some well over a century old — wear authentic costumes. They range in size from miniscule to life-sized (the latter a wax replica of Britain's first Queen Elizabeth). A handsome china doll four feet high is outstanding; reproductions of famous personages include one of Jenny Lind.

Doll collecting has become "high priority" among today's collectors, making suitable dolls for museum display costly and hard to find. But the ones shown here can captivate doll buffs, and even casual visitors spend an hour in the museum on the average.

There are a collection of antique china and models of the pistols used in the assassinations of Presidents Lincoln and McKinley on view also. But the drawing card here is the hundreds and hundreds of dolls. The modest fee buys visitors the opportunity to browse through the past at their leisure.

Friendly Eating Places

Road's End Dory Cove — the restaurant with the dory on top (of a high pole) — is north of Lincoln City on Logan Road just off Highway 101. In nearby Road's End Park traces of the road built by Phil Sheridan in the 1850's between coastal points and the Siletz Indian Agency 20 years before he became famous as a Civil War General can still be seen.

Seafoods are featured at Dory Cove, steaks are available, but it is the clam chowder that is irresistable. It's a fun place to eat — a chowder house that might have been designed for a Disney film, with timbers hung with nets and floats among the plants, macrame window treatments, and tables centered with miniature yellow buoys on which the menu is printed. Prices are on the reasonable side.

Pixie Kitchen, featuring foods at affordable prices, is straight out of Mother Goose. The Pixie gardens outside present a three-dimensional view guaranteed to delight children. This is one eatery that goes all out to provide a pleasant stop for the whole family. Travelers will have no trouble spotting it as they drive through town.

The Inn at Spanish Head, Oregon's luxury hotel that climbs a ten-story-high ocean cliff at Lincoln City, is renowned for superb dining in their restaurant overlooking the crashing surf.

Glassblowing has been transformed to fine art by the talents of Buzz Williams of **Alderhouse II**, Oregon's oldest glassblowing studio. He has refined the techniques of off-hand glass production and used it to create unique pieces in limited quantities as well as popular vases and containers.

Visitors are encouraged to watch as he teases the molten glass into works of art, designing as he goes. The basic ingredients of glass are lime, sand and soda, but he doesn't have to start from scratch with his creations. He often works with recycled glass, using chemicals to add color and strength to the finished pieces. A 2,000-degree gas-fired furnace, used to heat the glass, must be kept fired around the clock, since it requires roughly two days to push the temperature back to the required intensity once it has cooled.

An hour spent watching the artisan working at this craft, which goes back to the middle ages, twirling and shaping the glowing blobs of near-liquid glass at the end of his long hollow rod, evokes legends of alchemists. A mounting sense of excitement seems to transform observers into participants as an identifiable design emerges minute by minute. Truly, a glassblowing studio is not *visited*; it is *experienced*.

Alderhouse II is open to visitors from 10:00 am to 5:00 pm every day, March through November. It is located a half mile east of Highway 101 on Immonen Road (a pleasant shady drive), a short distance south of the Siletz River.

Salishan Lodge, recognized nationally as one of the Northwest's finest resorts, is located just south of Lincoln City at Gleneden Beach. The appointments are elegant; the accommodations are all-inclusive: an 18-hole on-grounds golf course and a children's playground; pool and sauna and a unisex gym; an art gallery and a beauty salon; all rooms with fireplaces and balconies providing superb ocean views. There are tennis courts and hiking trails, and agate beds nearby. Three fine restaurants are noted for excellent food: The **Gourmet Room**, the **Sun Room** coffee shop, and the **Cedar Tree** (summer).

The Marketplace at Salishan is a mall with style, with some two dozen shops, most open daily starting at 10:00 am. They are specialty shops for the most part — a shoppers' paradise in the round — where unusual gift, souvenir and personal items are to be expected. Impossible to list them all. Representative are **Between Friends**, where imports of style intermingle with quality regional arts, wicker and brass; **Up Against the Wall**, showing exceptional framed prints, mounted jasper and thundereggs, and other art gifts; **Lawrence Gallery** presenting works of fine Northwest artists in many mediums — painting, sculpture, weaving, glass and jewelry, carvings and ceramics.

Coast Roast Coffee Shop, featuring gourmet coffees roasted on the premises, fine teas, crumpets and bagels for carry-out or in-house consumption, and **Hot Pots**, displaying unusual and gourmet kitchen items, is connected by an archway, making it easy for shoppers with fastidious tastes to coordinate purchases.

The **Allegory Bookshop** has expanded the list of titles carried by several hundred, but browsers have no need to crane their necks scanning spine titles on tightly-packed shelves. Most books are displayed to show the covers in this airy shop where shelves and cases are arranged to allow views of trees and open space. This is a must stop for those who love good books.

The Marketplace Restaurant offers casual and comfortable lunching and dining with a lovely view of the bay, from 11:30 am every day. The seafood is very good, the sandwiches are whoppers, and the prices are affordable. A champagne brunch on Sundays — 10:00 am-2:00 pm — is a delightful extra.

Annual Events

Spring Kite Festival, "D" River Wayside, May.
Fall Kite Festival, "D" River Wayside, late September.
Clam Chowder Cook-Off, Lincoln City, October.
Driftwood Derby — horse races on the beach, Lincoln City, October.

Otter Crest Loop — a four-mile stretch of low, curving coast road not integrated into Highway 101 where it climbs the heights between Depoe Bay and Newport — should be a priority side trip for visitors to the Oregon coast. The paved narrow road is draped along the lower cliffs like a strip of tinsel on a Christmas tree, providing intimate glimpses of pounding surf and secluded beaches from between thick coastal vegetation supplemented by panoramas of the primitive coastline from informal turnouts along the way.

The high point of the drive, literally, is the large State of Oregon observation area atop **Cape Foulweather**, named in 1778 by Captain James Cook. This first encounter with the Pacific Coast of North America by the British explorer was frustrated by an ocean storm of such magnitude it almost forced him to abandon his search for the legendary Northwest Passage; a stretch which took him finally to Nootka Harbor at Vancouver Island in late March.

The weather at the cape supports its name. At times fog swirls in so thickly it is like walking inside a cloud of damp smoke. The high chain link fence which protects visitors from deep chasms on two sides, the forested cliffs, are obscured within minutes.

But on a clear day you can, indeed, seem to see forever. Powerful telescopes allow close-ups of coastal birds and the white sea lions which play on the rocks offshore at low tide.

On the very edge of the 500-foot promontory beside the parking area is **The Lookout Gift Shop and Observatory**, one of the best along the coast. Owners Kathryn and Ralph Peyton, for seventeen years operators of Oregon's Crater Lake Resort, travel extensively to seek out unusual articles from around the world for the shop.

The wide variety of quality gift items and art objects is evident as one steps into the shop, which seems to hang like a crow's nest over the ocean. Tiny figurines carved of semi-transparent stone from Russia's Ural Mountains shine with an inner luster highlighted by a finish treatment of hot paraffin.

Wooden bears from Hokkaido, Japan's far-northern island, are made by the remnants of the primitive Ainu tribe, of whom there are fewer than five hundred survivors.

Sharks, whales, and seals carved of ironwood from the Baja California desert by the Seri Indians are exquisite in their simplicity. The Seris, a stone-age tribe discovered only sixty years ago, have set up a production line for producing these flowing, satin smooth figures by hand. The members of the tribe — many of whom have never seen the animals they carve — block out the rough figures, which are then finished by the five master carvers of the tribe.

Shelves and cases are filled with special imported items: wood boxes decorated with enamel designs from Poland and woven water baskets from Africa compete for attention with jewelry from New Zealand shells of a radiant blue.

And that's only one part of the offerings to be found here. Bins and bins of seashells fill a small annex beneath collections of glass floats from one to twenty-four inches in diameter hanging from the ceiling timbers. These once-common beach finds are now collectors' items, traveling estimated distances up to 20,000 miles on ocean currents before being washed onto the coastal beaches.

The Lookout also features a marine museum which exhibits artifacts from wrecked ships which once carried supplies and goods for early traders and settlers in the Oregon country. A huge brass telescope estimated to be over a hundred years old has been in use at the shop since it was started in 1938.

The road continues on past the **Inn At Otter Crest**, one of the coast's superior resorts, whose timbered units cling to the hilly shoreline among the evergreens as if they too had dug deep roots into the rock cliffs.

The road, which begins at Whale Cove at the north end, rejoins the highway at the village of Otter Rock.

The Lookout Gift Shop on Cape Foulweather seems to hang like a crow's nest over the ocean, filled with unusual items from around the world. Shells in variety and quantity; marine brass; books by Northwest writers also find shelf space here. Telescopes mounted in the vista viewpoint area outside allow close-up looks at birds and sea lions on the rocks below. Cape Foulweather, named by Captain James Cook, whose ship was battered by a severe storm at this point, can be enveloped in a blanket of heavy fog without warning, its landmarks obscured within minutes. But on a clear day magnificent coastal views are visible for miles north and south.

DEPOE BAY

A historical market beside the bay describes the town's background. Indian Charlie Depot (so named for having worked at a United States Army Depot when Indians registered through the Siletz Agency were required to have English names for census rolls and recording of land holdings) was alloted lands around the Bay in 1894. The town was platted in 1927 and named DePoe — the family over the years having changed the spelling. When the post office was established the next year, the government further simplified the spelling at Depoe Bay, without the capital P.

Spouting horns along the rocky shore often send geysers shooting high into the air, on occasion squirting arches of water across the highway. But there is no predicting the timing of these natural displays, and visitors may be lucky enough to witness them any time of the year. Chances are best though in winter when ocean storms intensify breaker activity.

Things to See and Do

The flocks of seagulls using the jagged rocks at **Boiler Bay** Wayside as a launching pad for their wheeling flights over cascading waves seem unperturbed by the tides' assaults on the wild shoreline. Casual visitors often assume the name describes the ocean's frenzied activity here, until they discover the memorial sign which explains the bay is named for a boiler from a turn-of-the-century steam schooner, the **J. Marhoffer**, which burned off Cape Foulweather May 19, 1910.

The wooden steamer was turned into an inferno within minutes when a gas torch, in the hands of an assistant engineer unfamiliar with its workings, ignited in the engine room. The **Marhoffer's** Captain Gustav Peteron ordered the helmsman to head the blazing vessel toward shore as the two lifeboats were launched. With twenty-one crew members, the captain and his wife watched as the flaming ship crashed into the shore rocks and exploded.

Interpreting as a warning the signals of a woman who

ran to Fogarty Beach waving a red sweater to indicate a safe landing place, the survivors rowed two miles south to Whale Cove and landed safely. The ship's cook, badly burned, was the only casualty.

The rusty boiler eventually washed ashore at Boiler Bay. Now, burrowed into the sand, it is photographed by tourists, scoured by the tides, and is seemingly ignored by the gulls.

This is a pleasant stop for leg-stretching or lunch. There are twenty-five picnic tables and restrooms in the wayside, which offers spectacular scenic views of the ocean.

Depoe Bay is publicized as the world's smallest navigable harbor. But its six acres of water is headquarters for commercial and charter fishing fleets which rank among the finest on the Oregon coast. Completely equipped charter fishing boats offer deep sea trips, while excursions are available for sightseers.

The Tradewinds Trollers owned by Stan Allyn is representative of the accommodations afforded visitors who take advantage of the recreation offered through the Depoe Bay fleets. Deep sea charters begin at dawn and continue through the day, averaging four hours each, with longer trips planned by arrangement for groups of six or more.

Coffee and rain gear are provided, along with bait and tackle and fish bags. Icing and/or canning facilities are located in Depoe Bay for preserving the catch and making shipping arrangements also.

An angler's license for salmon (the only fish requiring one) can be obtained at the Tradewinds office on a daily basis. Those who take the trip as non-fishing passengers may go for half fare.

Forty-minute excursion trips around the bay are also available through Tradewinds, with children under six riding free. The scenic cruise may include a close-up view of whales during their migrations up and down the coast.

For confirmed landlubbers, the thrill of the catch may be

experienced vicariously by watching from the highway underpass viewpoints which overlook the docks as clients' catches are prepared for packing after each trip. The observation deck atop the Depoe Bay State Park building on the ocean side offers an excellent viewpoint for watching the Depoe Bay fleet boats enter and leave the harbor through the high rock walls of the narrow channel. Telescopes allow visitors to watch the boats far out from shore.

Harbor facilities here are easily accessible, and a wide variety of shops keeps visitors interested while waiting for cruises and fishing trips to begin.

Gift certificates are offered by Tradewinds and the other charter companies operating out of Depoe Bay: **Deep Sea Charters**, **Jimco Dock**, and **Pier I Sportfishing**.

An aquarium in a coastal town may seem redundant to the casual visitor. But travelers should not be misled into bypassing the **Depoe Bay Aquarium**. There are only two older aquariums in the United States. This one is truly, as its advertising proclaims, "like taking a walk on the floor of the ocean."

The exhibits are presented in a background which simulates an undersea cave. Fish appear and disappear in rock-framed "windows" in an ever-changing show of grace and motion. The 1,600 gallon fish tank includes starfish and crabs, sea urchins, and anemones among its large assortment of ocean creatures.

Large specimens are on display also: a green sea turtle, for instance (they sometimes grow to over 800 pounds); a wolf eel (an adult can snap a 2 x 4 with its jaws); several octupi which can change color at will (deep red to white or vice versa) by manipulating the pigment cells of their skins.

But the main attraction is the small herd of harbor seals that live in the tiled pool in the grotto. These personable creatures are born entertainers who delight spectators by the tricks they perform when thrown pieces of fish, on sale in small packets for this purpose. It's worth the modest admission price for the seals alone; the rest of the exhibit is a bonus.

On any sunny day—and often on stormy ones—the observation deck at the north end of the bridge at Depoe Bay is a
favorite spot for vacationers watching the activity in the
sheltered boat basin below. Charter boats depart and return
to the docks below where fish caught by the clients of
the deep-sea vessels are cleaned and packed in ice to be
carried home.

Shops and Marts in Depoe Bay

The Pacific Brass and Copper Works is just a tad off the highway but it's worth looking for. It's advertised as "the shiniest place on the Oregon coast" and you'd better believe it. Anything in brass and copper that the average traveler would find of interest can probably be found here, from nautical antiques to hardware. Visitors will have no trouble finding this shop next door to the old post office in Depoe Bay on the north side of the bridge. They're open four days a week — Wednesday through Sunday — 10:00 am to 6:00 pm.

Pink Panther Gifts has handmade Indian jewelry; **Spindrift Gifts** features collector chess sets from all over the world, both north of the bridge on the highway.

The handcrafted door to **Foxythings Gifts** looks like an outsized gift package. Weathered boards placed on the diagonal form a background for wood cutouts of flowers and letters attractively mounted to identify the shop and establish the tone for the unusual stoneware pieces found inside. Pottery wine sets — carafes and glasses — of distinctive design and colors are especially noteworthy. But many of the pieces shown at Foxythings have unique touches which set them apart from the purely utilitarian pottery.

Dining Out in Depoe Bay

The **North Point Cafe**, a small restaurant surrounded by window walls affords diners a wide-angle view directly into the bay. At low tide a recurrent pattern of shadows portrays a classic "Indian Brave" head in the shallow waters. Sea lions often frolic here to entertain patrons while their meals are being prepared. This is strictly a come-as-you-are eating spot, and it offers one of the loveliest views of the Depoe Bay waters.

The Sea Hag in the center of Depoe Bay is known up and down the coast for its food and entertainment. The newly decorated restaurant is inviting inside and out. They feature a Sunday Champagne Brunch, buffet specials during the week, and prime rib on Saturday nights; music for dancing from 8 pm. A fun place any day in the week.

Tucked away in a bend of the hilly coast highway a couple of miles south of Depoe Bay is a delightful motel/restaurant unit. **Whale Cove** is small, sitting among the trees on the edge of the cliffs overlooking a hidden inlet where the whales come in frequently to scrape the barnacles off against the steep rock walls on their way north. Rumor has it moonshiners once dumped a load of bourbon in the waters here to escape its being confiscated by government men.

Annual Events

The annual **Fleet of the Flowers** at Depoe Bay is held each Memorial Day. After special services, memorial wreaths are loaded onto boats which move slowly through the channel and out to sea where the flowers are tossed onto the ocean's surface as the boats parade in a circle around them to commemorate those from the area who have lost their lives at sea.

Each year in September a community **Indian Salmon Bake** is held at Fogarty State Park. Salmon baked on sticks thrust into the ground over fire trenches is served to the public at this yearly celebration of the salmon harvest.

Devil's Punchbowl between Depoe Bay and Newport is a natural marine "sculpture" carved by the surf crashing into the rocky cliffs. At high tide a great rock cauldron froths and whirls in the giant "punchbowl"; at low tide marine gardens can be explored. This exciting picnic area atop the ocean cliff has some two dozen picnic sites with stoves, and restrooms that include facilities for the handicapped. Trails lead down to the ocean beach at the base of the cliff for fishers and beachcombers to enjoy. A delightful setting for viewing, photographing, or relaxing in the sun when the "punchbowl" is dry.

Notes:

Areas typical of the lush forest lands inhabited by the northern coastal Indians before the coming of white settlers can still be enjoyed in many of the state's parks. Oswald West State Park 10 miles south of Cannon Beach offers both ocean beaches and rain forest woods, plus 36 primitive camp sites.

The Indians

The Indians of the Oregon coast were different from their inland neighbors—lighter-skinned, finer-boned, who bathed often, cleaned their cedar-plank houses regularly and changed their beds by placing fresh evergreen boughs between new woven mats. They were boatmen instead of horsemen; harvesters instead of hunters.

Early explorers named them "flatheads," seeing most of the Salish and Chinook with flattened foreheads. Some bands shaped heads to a point in back; others forced them into a shelved ridge shape. But not all coast tribes practiced head shaping, and all had given it up by the late 1800's.

The salmon, food staple of the coastal Indians, was inter-woven through their culture. As late as the 1940's a secret salmon festival was being held each year by Indians along the Columbia. Present-day Siletz Indians, seeking to recover from the federal government reservation lands surrounding the site of their former Indian Agency, have asked spe-cifically to be awarded "a few hundred salmon a year for cultural purposes" in addition to the land.

Before wagon trails and railroads opened the coast valleys to public access, the Indian population was made up of bands, extensions of a dozen larger families. Languages spoken by these scattered bands were so diverse that when remnants of the groups were exiled to the reservation at Siletz in 1856, it was necessary for many of them to learn jargon—a mixture of Chinook, French, and English words which had become the *lingua franca* of the early Northwest—before they could understand each other.

Families varied in size from a few dozen persons to

several hundred. Thirty-six bands of the Chinook family lived along the south side of the Columbia; the Kusan family at Coos Bay had only three bands. The groups lived together without too much conflict. Their "wars" were often arranged by agreement between chiefs of the bands involved.

When Dr. John McLaughlin took over as governor of the Hudson Bay Company holdings at Fort Vancouver in 1825, he administered the profitable "fur preserve" and its inhabitants sternly but fairly for his time. But with the increasing immigration to the northwest during the next 15 years, stimulated by a depression in the United States, and spearheaded by the overland crossings of the missionaries, unrest began to grow among the Indians. The massacre at Wailatpu Mission near Walla Walla, in which missionary Doctor Marcus Whitman and his wife Narcissa were killed, set off a decade of conflict between settlers and natives of the Oregon Territory.

The grievances were heightened on both sides by the epidemic of gold fever which spread from California along the rivers of the Oregon border, and by the infiltration of settlers into the lush coastal lands, eager to stake claims there. The coast Indians were caught up in the resulting conflicts and in 1856 were literally herded onto reservations, either as a result of treaties (few of them honored) or as prisoners of war.

Some were taken to the reservation at Grande Ronde; most ended up at the Siletz reservation. Soldiers routed Indians from their homes, without warning in many cases, at the end of the Rogue wars, marching them to the new lands without provisions. With no household possessions, and the foreign names arbitrarily assigned to make record keeping easier for the agents, their traditional family groups were broken up.

From the beginning white settlers moved onto Indian lands almost as they chose, aided by government agencies which found means to remove the natives from their choice acres. The Siuslaws, who originally owned more than 500,000 acres along the Siuslaw River, were maneuvered into signing a treaty with the United States government in 1855 which specified payment in full of an agreed sum for their property. As late as 1970 payment had not been made.

With the formation of the Siletz reservation—a little over a million acres—many of the Siuslaws were transplanted there along with what was left of other family groups. But within 20 years these lands, too, had been placed in public domain and opened to homesteaders, except for areas close around the agency site. After the agency was closed in 1929, the Indians, many of whom homesteaded their own lands in the area, were gradually absorbed into the community. When the United States government formally terminated the Confederated Indian Tribes of the Siletz in 1954, the tribes no longer existed.

But in 1967 steps were begun to resurrect the Siletz tribal entity, and in 1977 they became the second tribe in the nation to achieve restoration. On September 3, 1980 the Siletz Indian Reservation Act was signed by President Carter, transferring 3,360 acres of federal lands, once part of the original Coast Reservation, to the tribe. In addition, the city of Siletz is restoring to them the 36-acre Agency site at Government Hill, which includes the Indian Cemetery trans- ferred to the Tribal Association in 1975.

The restoration of status as a tribe was pushed partly to make the Siletz peoples eligible for education, medical and social benefits, and job training under government programs. But leaders emphasize that acquisition of the reservation will also help restore and preserve the cultural heritage which is fast being lost as individuals are absorbed into a white society.

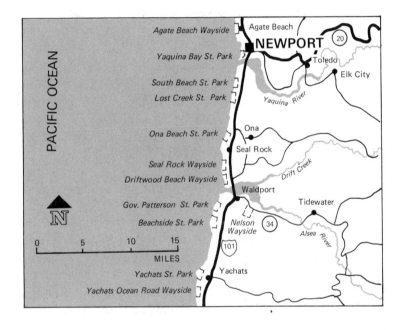

Newport
Waldport

NEWPORT

As with many coastal towns, Newport's waterfront seems to hum with a special energy. This is where most coastal settlements have their beginnings; where historic buildings are often found; where rejuvenation usually begins as veteran buildings that have survived the assaults of wind and storms imposed by accumulating years are remodeled to house new enteprises.

Newport's **Old Town** bayfront is a fascinating combination of past and future. Modern art galleries, antique and gift shops rub shoulders with seafood markets, tackle shops and charter ramps. A picture-book US Coast Guard station vies with picturesque scenes and landmark buildings for the attention of photographers.

Colorful charter boats line up at their docks in Yaquina Bay like toys at the edge of a pond. The festive paint and trim lines are deceiving; however, these are the vessels which carry fishing parties out across the harbor bar to fish deep waters in hopes of experiencing the excitement of pulling in "big ones."

Newport Sportfishing is based at the Embarcadero dock, and offers full service for fishing devotees: from 24-hour phone service for reservations to payment by credit card; bait and tackle required; trips ranging from 4 through 12 hours; group and senior citizen discounts. They also provide dive and whale-watching trips, and sailboat excursions.

Also operating from Bay Boulevard docks are **Sea Gull Charters**, **Newport Tradewinds**, and **Cape Perpetua Seafoods and Charters**.

Free coffee while on board is standard. No license is required for bottom fishing; charters can supply needed licenses for salmon fishing.

On around Bay Boulevard, where it merges with Moore Drive, is **The Embarcadero**, Newport's fine resort/marina. The Embarcadero offers condominium-style accommodations: one- and two-bedroom apartments with fireplace and kitchen, plus studio units, at prices that are well in line with local motels. The problem may lie in obtaining reservations.

The Embarcadero's excellent moorage facilities can handle any craft from outboards to cruisers. Beautifully situated for vacation fishing (your boat or theirs from their rental fleet), the marina is popular with those wishing to relax and fish with the least hassle possible. Rental service includes all needed gear for clamming and crabbing, as well as for fishing.

Recreation facilities include play areas for children, a swimming pool, sauna, and whirlbath. Outdoor fishing piers are complete with cleaning stations, plus barbecues and crab cookers for outdoor parties.

It's just minutes away from beaches and coastal attractions, offering every convenience for the family vacation (except housing pets) or convention gatherings.

Gift shops and galleries are staples of resort towns, and Old Town Newport is no exception. The many fine shops are worth exploring.

The Wood Gallery stands tall on Bay Boulevard at 8th Street. This one is a must if you can't browse them all. It's classy and spendy and quality all the way, featuring the works of the Northwest's outstanding artists and artisans. Truly distinctive pottery is displayed to advantage, uncrowded and separated so that no style competes with another. Stunning framed art photography by Reinhold Schabe and batiks by Pat Rutledge capture the attention immediately.

Especially lovely are small lamps with designer shades in stained glass—some with price tags that edge up to four figures. Marine paintings, carvings, glass pieces catch the eye. Somehow, everything in the spacious gallery seems to be one of a kind, and different in a very special way.

B & C Gallery carries a variety of gift and souvenir items. Of note are blown glass figurines—individual pieces numbered and registered—and hand-crafted jewelry.

At **The Sea Chest** look for nautical brass and metal sculpture along with other gift items.

Aunt Belinda's Salt Water Taffy Shop, as colorful as the confections for which it is known, offers three dozen or so flavors of the chewy candy, plus a tempting variety of other goodies from around the world.

The Underseas Gardens on the bay in Newport is, literally, a floating aquarium; one big half-million gallon tank wrapped around the viewing room. The more than 5000 exhibits—most from the coastal waters around Newport—have attracted millions of visitors. And there are added attractions to make this something more than a run-of-the-mill aquarium. An underseas diver is on hand to point out the marine animals as they are described by a narrator. The gardens are open daily 10:00 am to 5:00 pm (9:00 pm summers) major holidays excepted. Young and old will find this "garden at the bottom of the sea" a fascinating experience.

Mariner Square

This recent monomall addition to the bayfront is a multi-level complex of passages and courtyards and sea-gray buildings housing **The Wax Works**—the supermodern reincarnation of the venerable Royal Pacific Wax Museum that was for years a prime tourist attraction in uptown Newport—and its attendant enterprises.

To enter this house of marvels is to step through a time warp that presents antiquity, recent history, and space-age future side by side. The depictions of nature's wonderments are interspersed with presentations of imaginative forays into future centuries. Models of famous personages, noted and notorious, are viewed in appropriate settings that make these "living museum" scenes realistic enough to pass for originals.

The subjects are manifold. Wagon train pioneers struggle over trails within shouting distance of space travelers; criminals are posed in perpetration of their crimes. And the mirrored hall that backdrops the dramatization of The Sermon On The Mount reflects an awesome solemnity.

Exiting from this "universe of the imagination" into the complex **Gift Shop** is anticlimactic, but here too are displayed small wonders of a different sort: outstanding greeting card assortments, some designs displayed in frames, for instance; brass trinket boxes and sculptures in marine motifs—animals, anchors and shells. Small plug-in nightlights made from sea shells are charming and inexpensive, representative of similar items carried here at reasonable prices.

The Whale's Tale not only serves up delicious food; the unusual decor is a visual delight of matching caliber. Among their specialties is poppy seed pancakes served with honey, and omelets of high reputation. Breakfast is served beginning at 7:00 am; dinner is served until 9:00 pm on weekends.

Canyon Way Restaurant and Bookstore is a short walk up Canyon Way Drive from the bayfront. The food here is very special; the bookstore is a treasurehouse of quality volumes on almost any subject.

Newport Waterfront

MO's, the little chowder house begun years ago by a fisherman's wife to have hot food waiting at the wharf when the fishing boats came in, proudly boasts, "We're not fancy but we're famous!" And indeed they are. The fame of Mo's clam chowder has spread—branches in Lincoln City, Florence, and Coos Bay bear witness—to the point where the original site has been supplemented by two annexes. These are informal places. Guests sit on benches at trestle tables wherever they can crowd in, because Mo's is usually crowded. Chowder is only the beginning of the good food served here. Louis-type salads are piled high with shrimp or crab; the slumgullion is something to rave about, and they bake a blackberry cobbler that would make grandmother turn green with envy.

And Up On The Hill

Sea Towne is a complex formed of buildings joined by walks and verandas and open stairways to create the ultimate in "courtyard" shopping, landscaped to compliment the patio design. Two dozen shops and businesses are housed here, many open daily, including clothing and shoe stores, galleries and gift and specialty shops, a beauty salon, and rest rooms.

The Champagne Patio tucked in along one wall of **Swafford's Oregon Specialties** is a delightful "lunch and tea room" type eatery featuring Swedish recipes prepared by Christina Swafford. Desserts are the melt-in-your-mouth kind; the Swedish bread is delicious; the coffee is strong and hot; house wine can be ordered by the glass.

Swafford's specialties include fine Oregon foods and wines, plus a good selection of imported wines as well; a deli case along one wall is filled with take-home foods attractive enough to star in *Bon Appetit*.

The pace here is relaxed, the dining area is charming, the people are friendly, making this a very pleasant spot for enjoying lunch or dessert.

The Lincoln County Historical Museum looks like one. The old log cabin exhibits the usual articles that chronicle a region's history: household goods, tools, machinery, and of course marine artifacts. Items in the fine Indian collection, mostly from those who came to be known as Siletze after being transplanted from many coastal areas to the Siltez Agency lands, were acquired from a former storekeeper who worked at the agency in the 1880's.

Hilan's Castle

A resort town on the Oregon Coast may seem to be an unlikely site for a Welsh castle, but it's there, overlooking the Pacific near Nye Beach, and has been for more than 70 years. Built in 1913 by photographer Charles Roper and his wealthy wife, Theresa, it was the most imposing house in the area in the years preceding World War I.

It is believed to be a replica of Highland Castle in Newport, Wales; the plans reportedly drawn from a photograph of its Scottish namesake built shortly after the Norman Conquest in the 13th Century. But with the passing years Newport's "Highland Castle" has become known as "Hilan's" Castle.

The four-story structure has had an up-and-down history since the days when its splendor was the talk of the town. Its 20 rooms represented the ultimate in luxury at the time of its completion—$4000 worth, to be exact. The upper floor, roofed with glass skylights and graced by a round turret room, served as Roper's studio. There he specialized in portraits of soldiers stationed in Newport during the first World War, along with scenic views of the dramatic coast landscapes surrounding the town.

His wife Theresa—described as *eccentric* and *romantic* by those who knew her—pursued a career as a writer in the conservatory, a room walled in glass and filled with plants and her several collections. Her claim to prominence was based on a historical novel she authored, *Rebounding Vengeance,* based on the Indian legend of Jumpoff Joe. The couple's only child, Georgiana, occupied the floor below the studio along with a large dollhouse and more than 100 dolls.

The Ropers were forced to sell the castle in 1930 due to financial reverses, and the building gradually retrogressed from imposing mansion in the 1930's to a low-rental boarding house in the late 1970's. But the old castle is now being restored and proposed for listing in the National Registry of Historic Places.

Although it is not open to the public, the building is worth driving past. It is situated just off Highway 101 to the west on 5th Street. The most striking view, however, is to be seen traveling uphill from the beach, especially in late afternoon with the sun highlighting the crenelated roofline and turret room.

The Bay Bridge Mall is a neat and inviting minimall at the north end of the bridge, anchored by **The Bridge Company**, a "full service" restaurant, breakfast through dinner, seven days a week.

The Normandie features "gifts for all occasions" and they are there in variety. One section is devoted to teddy bear specialties. In addition to a charming assortment of the cuddly toys, they carry such TB novelty items as bear paperdolls with cut-out clothes, bear posters to delight younger children, and bear books.

In another area a shelf case is filled with music boxes and figurines of carousel figures and groupings. Exquisite workmanship, these painted carousel animals will delight collectors and children alike. They range in price from $25 to $350—the latter a complete carousel that whirls to the music from a wind-up music box. Greeting cards and books are available here too, plus jewelry and novelties and carvings and—well, gifts for all occasions.

Other businesses at the location include **Capehouse** (gourmet kitchen shop) and **Bay Bridge Needlework**.

The **Hatfield Marine Science Center** encompasses many programs. To the quarter-million visitors who follow the curving road under the Yaquina Bay Bridge to the center's complex on the Bay each year, it appears to be a combination of museum and aquarium. It is that, and much more.

The exhibits section is open daily the year around for "window views" of Oregon's marine life and close-up inspections of historical displays of diving suits, telescopes, and other nautical gear. In the middle of the lobby is a touching pool where youngsters (oldsters too if they wish) are encouraged to get the feel of some of the sea creatures that thrive along Oregon's coast. There's an opportunity for anyone so inclined to get close to an octopus, too, within limits.

The center's bookstore carries a fine assortment of printed materials relating to coastal subjects. The halls around the courtyard often serve as displays for regional artists and photographers. Vacationers to the area can time their visits to coincide with the Seatauqua Summer Program, sponsored each year by Oregon State University, offering lectures, films, workshops, tours and other activities to involve and inform participants in coastal lore.

South Beach Charters is a full-service marina; a "deluxe" facility with RV accommodations, restrooms and showers, parking for hundreds of vehicles, and slips for hundreds of sea craft. They charter diving, excursion and fishing trips—even an overnighter—furnishing gear, licenses, and lunches for clients. They offer a lot of extras here.

Annual Events

Loyalty Day has been observed in Newport the weekend nearest May 1 annually for over 20 years.

The Seafood and Wine Festival, sponsored by the Chamber of Commerce, is held the weekend nearest Washingtons birthday.

The Blessing of the Fleet, a ceremony held in early March in memory of persons lost at sea, is sponsored by the Fishermen's Wives Association.

Toledo Loop Trip

A delightful drive begins from Old Town, following Bay Boulevard around the bay to where it connects with Yaquina Bay Road just past The Embarcadero. Marina docks are tucked against the shoreline at intervals along the rustic river.

Mini middens of chalky shells mark the site of **Oregon Oyster Company**, the 67-acres oyster farm founded almost 80 years and still operated by members of the Wachsmuth family. During the summer, July-September, the farm goes "fallow" as the warming waters of the bay render the oysters unpalatable. But the rest of the year shuckers open the shells at the rate of 2000-4000 each per day.

Riverbend Moorage is a supermarina with RV hookups as well as mooring slips, where vacationers can purchase tackle and hardware, groceries, licenses and propane. There's a mobile home park on the rise above the docks.

The turnaround point is at historic **Toledo**, a mill town that grew around the holdings of two homesteaders at the site in 1865.

Turn-of-the-century homes are scattered through the town. A 1911 log house is still in use up the hill on First Street.

To continue the loop, backtrack past the point where Yaquina Bay Road enters town and cross Highway 20 for a 5-mile drive to **Siletz** and **Government Hill**, once more the center of a **Siletz Indian Reservation**. A modern community center building centers the park area where federal agency buildings stood when the reservation housed native Americans who's tribal lands had been preempted by homesteaders and settlers. Lodge poles stacked at an angle—butts on the ground, tips in the limb crotches of park trees—are reminiscent of shelters used by those forced to provide their own housing, without tools or materials, after the long march to the strange reservation in the 1850's.

Return to Newport via Highway 20. Round-trip driving distance is roughly 30 miles; the time can vary from an hour to a day, depending on the curiosity quotient of the travelers.

SEAL ROCK

Seal Rock is the terminal of the Corvallis/Yaquina Bay wagon road, the first to link the coast with the interior valleys of the state. Hidden behind the picnic area of **Seal Rock Wayside** three miles north of Waldport is one of Oregon's most delightful beaches. Protected to the north by titanic cliffs and monoliths, the small beach manages to retain an air of seclusion. There's usually someone fishing from the rocks at low tide, silhouetted against sea and sky. The clamming is excellent here. Artists sometimes perch on convenient overhangs trying to capture in sketches the restless beauty of waves crashing against rocks and invading the chasms among the roots of the rock cliffs. Hikers can't resist the narrowing bridge of cliff sand which scoots up to the top of the highest rocks. And photographers can't resist the chance to photograph these adventurers outlined against the sky.

The community of Seal Rock has its fair share of artists and craftspeople, and an unusual tourist attraction. There's no way travelers along Highway 101 can miss **Sea Gulch** where it sits on a rise like some forgotten relic of the Old West; it's the **Trading Post** surrounded by a yardful of near-lifesized carvings of western characters created by chain saws. **The Outback**—6 acres of forest land peopled by carved wood frontier characters—includes a Boot Hill exhibit. Often demonstrations of chain-saw carving are given for onlookers. This is a fun trip for kids and adults alike; sort of like being lost in a cartoon strip, but it makes a nice break in the day.

For those more attuned to the arts, **Seal Rock Art Gallery** displays the works of area artists and artisans, from classic to experimental. A large gallery room shows paintings, photography and prints in variety; in the entry room are unusual sculptures, figurines, hangings and such.

The Calico Kitchen is a comfortable eatery specializing in "homemade" foods in keeping with their "handmade" decor. It is a favorite of residents in the area, recommendation enough for those traveling through or visiting.

WALDPORT

Waldport, situated in an area once encompassed by the Siletz Indian Reservation, was opened to white settlers in 1875, who promptly panned $1,700 in gold dust from the beach sands nearby. In 1881 the post office was established, and three years later the town was platted, the streets laid out by the stars. Today Waldport is developing into a choice retirement town. The moderate weather, leisurely pace, fine fishing, plus excellent community facilities make this an ideal location for retirees. The population hovers around 1000, but may change as more and more people find their way to the little coast town where, in the past, there's been "plenty of nothing" to do, and plenty of time to get it done without hurrying. The signs point to growth and expansion, with new businesses popping up like mushrooms. New docks on the bayfront are a boon to fishing enthusiasts.

There's something new at **Trident Antiques**, recognized as one of the coast's largest and best antique emporiums for the past decade. The fine old pieces of polished, carved wood accented with marble and glass still hold the spotlight. But another area has been added, featuring "antiques of the future" created by regional designers and craftspeople. Even the bears (a requiste for gift shops everywhere these days) are out of the ordinary — limited edition Executive Teddy Bears from Collectables Creations are elegantly clothed in velveteen suits. An array of distinctive designer soft sculpture includes plump geese from small to larger-than-life-sized; and mini stuffed rocking horses a few inches high made of striped ticking.

A corner is latticed off as an **Oregon Wine Room**, where Oregon wines and specialty food products are available. One delicacy not often available is authentic Scottish shortbread made by a local lady who makes the goodies from "old Country" family recipes.

The Seastrand Plaza on Highway 101 at the south end of town is a covered mall housing several businesses including **The Pizza Port**, and **Captain Squeeky's Laundry** — self-service or drop-off. **The Waldport Town Center** mini-mall a few blocks east on Highway 34 is the location of **International Burgers & Seafood**, a casual eating house featuring good foods with international flavors at very good prices; **Mosey's Furniture**, where interesting accessories — ceramic harp sculptures, for instance — accent the fine furnishings; plus others. Both of these complexes are recent additions to the town's enterprises.

Also new is **Jak's**, a "customer's choice" pizza shop with house pizzas offered in three sizes (10½, 13½, 15½ inches); or build-your-own and add your toppings, thick or thin crusts from their own special dough, for take-out baking. Call ahead or wait your turn. These are superlative pizzas at prices hard to believe. Jak's is located next door to **The Continental Deli** just south of the bridge on the highway.

An above average gift shop is located nearby — in the **Waldport Rexall Drugstore**. That's right! Unique greeting cards from several companies featuring distinctive designs are displayed here. But that's just the beginning. Some "different" gifts (not easy to find in an area where gift and craft shops flourish) noted here, for instance: deep red psuedo "glass" apples, lightweight and low priced; pastel baskets with mini baby dolls made from baby anklets, charming and affordable. They also have a comprehensive magazine counter, and a full line of art supplies.

Across the street at the **Waldport Yarn and Book Shop** can be found varieties of specialty yarns, from finest gauge to outsized jumbos, along with standard types, in a rainbow assortment of colors. A complete stock of accessories is carried here, plus patterns and instruction manuals. The book part of the shop is a wall given over to a paperback exchange counter.

Kozy Kove Marina, 9½ miles east of Waldport on the Alsea River has all the standard requirements for river fishing: boats and launch ramp, trailer, RV, and tent spaces, a general store. It also has a special extra: a floating restaurant on the Alsea River where "fishing folk" can enjoy a hearty breakfast, vacationers can savor lunch, and coastal residents can drive out for special dinners on the covered dock rocking gently on the night-lighted river. Basics include steak, ribs, seafood and chicken dinners; daily lunch specials, clam chowder and homemade pies, Mexican and Italian foods. Kozy Kove is a pleasant 15-minute drive (you may want to dawdle a little along this coastal river road) and easy to spot. Just watch for the Old Captain wood sculpture on the river bank where the steps lead down to the restaurant. The atmosphere is serene, the food is excellent, and the prices are right.

The graceful waves and trenches of the 50-mile stretch of dunes which make up Oregon's "Sahara by the Sea" seem to echo the motion of the cresting ocean waves. From 2½ to 4 miles wide, the dunes advance inland up to six feet a year. Shaped by the wind in ever-changing patterns, this dune area contains some of the world's highest sand formations. Fresh-water lakes which are scattered through the sand hills were created by the advancing dunes damming up small streams. Areas of the Oregon dunes are open for camping and exploration.

The Dunes

Oregon recreationists have one of the world's largest sand piles at their doorstep: 32,000 acres of majestic dunes stretching almost 50 miles along the coast between Florence and Coos Bay. Since 1972 this enormous area of sand hills—two and a half to four miles wide—has been incorporated into the Oregon Dunes National Recreation Area designated for public enjoyment.

This active coastal area, ever-changing as the sea, advances north and east at approximately 6 feet a year. Sections have been stabilized by plantings of beach grass, shore pine, and the beautiful Scotch broom which, in season, splashes the coast landscape with sun-yellow blossoms where highways, channels, and other permanent installations must be protected from the encroaching areas.

The growth process of the dunes is a continuing cycle. The underlying sandstone base of the Oregon Coast Range mountains, perpetually eroded by the coastal climate, is whirled off to the ocean during spring flooding, only to drift back to land on westerly currents. The sand formations parallel the tidal action of the ocean, lapping in waves across the shore and building to spectacular heights. The world's largest sand dune rises to 380 feet in the Woahink Lake area near Florence.

The dunes are sprinkled with clear, sparkling, fresh-water lakes, as if a giant had tossed a handful of emeralds and aquamarines at random across its surface. Along the eastern edge of the recreation area the famous "fishing lakes" sprawl. Most of them bear Indian names: Woahink (Clear Lake), Tahkenitch (Lake of Many Arms), Cleawox (Lake in the Dunes) among them. Woahink Lake is indeed a clear deep blue; fed by fresh-water springs, it serves as the water supply for residences around its edges. To the west of the highway is Lake Cleawox, site of Lane County's Girl Scout Camp, divided by the ONDRA boundary; and one of the "many arms" of Tahkenitch Lake reaches inside the line.

Clear Lake, south of Reedsport, borders the highway. This is the only fenced lake in the group, and recreational use here is prohibited. A short distance farther, Eel Lake curls in a tight sickle shape, with the twin Tenmile Lakes fitting around and below it.

The lakes, large and small, were formed by sand dunes blocking the channels of streams in their relentless march inland. Over the centuries they have also smothered a giant evergreen forest, except for small islands of trees which show here and there among the ridges.

The dunes, like the sea, appear deceptively benign. People using the area are cautioned about some of the hazards which are ever-present, especially for children. Bulletins and signs remind vacationers that the sand near popular regions can contain broken glass and other debris which is buried by the shifting landscape; that it is easy to become lost in the dunes where wind action can wipe out footprints in an instant, and fog often creeps in swiftly; that dense undergrowth can cause panic, especially near dusk; that dry tips of beach grass can cut like razors; and that areas at the base of high mounds can be dangerous if dune buggies are in the vicinity.

Specific areas of the dunes are closed to vehicle traffic. One near Florence and another in northern Coos County prohibit vehicles from May through September; others are reserved for pedestrians the year around, including 3,000 acres of the highest dunes located in the Umpqua Scenic Area below Winchester Bay.

Campers are also cautioned about care with campfires. Dunes vegetation is full of oil and a fire, once started, can spread over large sections within minutes.

The dunes area is bracketed by Horsfall Beach, one of the longest on the coast, near Coos Bay; and by Honeyman State

Park, one of the area's loveliest, to the north at Florence. Honeyman has tent, trailer, and improved camping sites in abundance, plus all recreational facilities which include over 100 picnic sites in the beautifully maintained park.

The dunes area is under the jurisdiction of the United States Forest Service, with headquarters at 855 Highway Avenue, Reedsport, OR 97467.

The dunes overlook ten miles below Florence maintained by the US Forest Service comprises a complex of walkways, stairs and observation decks that provide scenic overviews of dunes and ocean. Picnic sites and restrooms make this a delightful "break" stop for those traveling the coast highway.

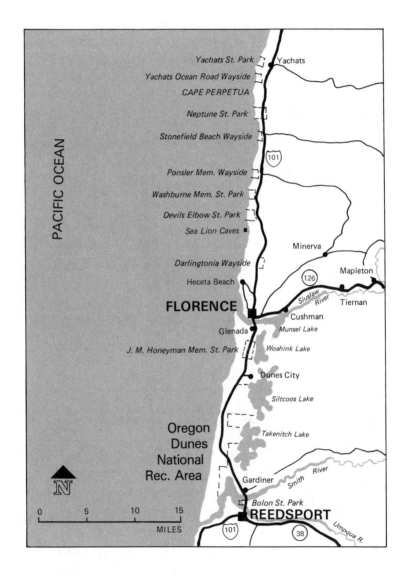

Yachats St. Park
Yachats
Yachats Ocean Road Wayside
CAPE PERPETUA
Neptune St. Park
Stonefield Beach Wayside
PACIFIC OCEAN
101
Ponsler Mem. Wayside
Washburne Mem. St. Park
Devils Elbow St. Park
Sea Lion Caves
Minerva
Darlingtonia Wayside
Mapleton
Heceta Beach
126
Siuslaw River
Tiernan
FLORENCE
Cushman
Glenada
Munsel Lake
J. M. Honeyman Mem. St. Park
Woahink Lake
Dunes City
Siltcoos Lake
Oregon
Dunes
National
Rec. Area
Takenitch Lake
Smith River
N
Gardiner
Bolon St. Park
0   5   10   15
REEDSPORT
MILES
101
38
Umpqua R.

Yachats
Florence
Reedsport

YACHATS

Yachats (pronounced Yah-hots) is a jewel of a vacation village snuggled up at the base of the coastal hills on the north shore of a small promontory which brackets the mouth of its namesake river. The tiny town of five hundred people reflects a pleasing blend of resort/retirement community. While tourism is a vital element in its survival, there is little of the obviously commercial development in evidence.

The pleasures offered vacationers here are those provided by sandy beaches, small coves, convenient fishing sites, quality shops, and excellent restaurants and motels, all somewhat understated. Yachats is one of the places on the coast where vacationers come to "get away from it all" rather than to "be where the action is." People retire here for the same reasons. It is quality, not quantity, that is offered here.

The headquarters of the Coast Range Indian Reservation was located here during the mid 1800's, and the area contains shell mounds which accumulated over hundreds of years at the ceremonial meeting places of the coast Indian bands. Unfortunately they are disappearing as more and more people discover the serendipities of retiring near the sea.

Interesting Places

The Devil's Churn Wayside three miles south of Yachats is a deep chasm in the shoreline where the tides thunder and crash against the rocky walls to froth like whipping cream. Walkways and railed paths lead down to observation points close to the churning activity through shady forest groves, with panoramic views of the coastline from the high points.

The **Cape Perpetua Visitor Center** dispenses information which will help visitors understand and appreciate the Oregon coast: geologically, historically, and esthetically. It is a focal point to coordinate the wonders of nature which surround this area of the coast in ways that will allow travelers and vacationers to enjoy these natural phenomena on their own.

In the 47-seat auditorium at the center, a short motion picture entitled "Forces of Nature" details the drama of the rocky headlands and sandy coves shaped by the relentless assaults of wind and water against the shore, and of the creatures which inhabit this area. Dioramas highlight the history of human beings and their effect upon the area.

A receptionist on duty at the information desk will answer questions and suggest points of interest to be enjoyed. A promenade deck offers a panoramic view; restrooms and drinking fountains are here too.

Trails with poetic names lead out from the center. The **Trail of the Restless Waters** goes to the **Devil's Churn**; the **Trail of the Whispering Spruce** takes visitors 800 feet above sea level; **Saint Perpetua Trail** goes to the highest point of the cape. And there are others. . . .

A self-guided auto tour turns off from the road above the visitor center that leads to the top of the cape, twisting and turning and climbing along a narrow paved road (most surely a revamped logging road) through lovely forest areas to the top of the ridge littered with felled skeletons of trees. Forest Service signs which blend with the natural background indicate special areas of trees and flowers.

The road roller-coasts for twenty-two miles through

A stroll on the beach at the ocean's edge as late afternoon shadows lengthen and early evening mists begin to roll in is one of the most pleasurable activities for coast visitors; a soothing alternative to the hustle-bustle of today's busy life.

forested hills before rejoining the highway at Yachats. This is truly a breathtaking ride, and for those uncourageous souls who retreat in the early stages, the downhill retracing offers some spectacular glimpses of blue sea far below, framed by forest giants that seem to stretch hundreds of feet before touching paler sky.

The visitor center is located in the Siuslaw National Forest of 620,000 acres, one of the few national forests which includes a seacoast. An entrance a fourth of a mile north is the start of the auto tour and cape loop drive, and also leads to the **Cape Perpetua Campground** with facilities for both picnicking and overnight camping.

The cape, highest point on the Oregon Coast, was named by English explorer Captain James Cook March 7, 1778, for Saint Perpetua who was martyred in Carthage March 7, 203 A.D., for professing her belief in Christianity.

The Muriel O. Ponsler Wayside is a small park fenced by a low stone wall which bears the marks of the masonry work provided by the Civilian Conservation Corps, the "army" of young men who enlisted in the CCC during the Depression of the 1930's. The land was donated to the state by Jack Ponsler for "public use and enjoyment" as a memorial to his wife. A few picnic tables, rather secluded, offer serene vistas of the ocean. An ornamental drinking fountain centers the park area, and through the years old-fashioned violets, wild strawberries, and daisies have spread to form a carpet of wildflowers in the spring. This is a delightful spot for lunching.

A couple of miles down the road toward Florence, **Carl G. Washburne State Park**, both sides of the highway, has some of the most inviting trailer sites among the coast's many lovely state parks. Low coast pines form green walls around spaces to give them a wonderful feeling of privacy. Winding forest roads through the park add to this sense of remoteness although neighbors may be right next door. A community kitchen and bathhouse are on the west side of the highway.

Trails from the east side sector lead through the woods to the beach. The campgrounds offer fifty-eight trailer spaces with utility hookups, two tent sites and nine picnic locales.

Shops and Such

Products of Ken and Herta Koogler, operators of **The Myrtletree** just north of Yachats are displayed in a pleasant showroom that fronts the factory. The former cabinetmaker designs graceful wood tableware and home accessories assisted by his wife. Much of it is finished in softer sheens that have replaced the high-lacquer finishes popular in earlier years. Myrtlewood requires special care in curing so that several years must elapse between harvest and manufacture. But the results can be worth waiting for, as evidenced here. Plates and bowls and trays are standards in myrtlewood; vases and desk sets and carvings (myrtlewood mushrooms are delightful!), boxes and jewelry are special. Small wood seals and whales with magnets are fun souvenir items. Shell trimmed candles in myrtlewood holders are lovely. They are open year around.

The Tole Tree is a combination gallery, gift shop and studio, specializing in tole painting but in no way limited to it. Instruction in the craft is available, and tole art pieces are for sale in the shop—handcrafted butterflies, tole painted, colorful as rainbows, for instance. But other craft gift items are plentiful too, from delicate imported ceramic boxes to carved wood holders—scissors and pencils—in the shape of loggers boots laced with leather thongs. A good place to look for "different" gifts to suit different tastes.

Yachats Gift Shop on the right coming into town is filled with small gift items reminiscent of the souvenir shops that have all but vanished today. Brass maritime figures for ornaments or hangings or hooks, boxes, and novelty toys—soft rubber seagulls that squeak like the live ones. And shells galore: carved shells from India, painted shells from local craftspeople, carved shell rings, are just a few of the fun things that are to be found here. And the prices are right in line.

Shirley's Country Creations specializes in quality hand-designed toys, doll clothes, baby and children's items not found just anywhere. Hand sewn, hand crocheted, hand knitted are norm here. This shop has to be browsed to appreciate the workmanship evidenced in these articles. Personalized hand-crafted designer dolls can be ordered here, faces reproduced from photographs; clothes meticulously hand-fashioned. These would make enchanting birthday gifts for young children—the kind that doting grandmothers bestow.

The Sea Fair Gift Shop where the highway right-angles toward the bridge offers a quality selection of works produced by Oregon artists and craftspeople. Smooth-flowing marine sculptures carved from coastal woods compete for attention with dramatic ink drawings, clocks made of driftwood, hand-printed notes and photography. Scrimshaw jewelry is exquisite; small shiny wood sculptures are delightful. A good selection of coastal books is carried also. It's a friendly place for looking and shopping.

Estimable Eateries

The dining room at **The Adobe**, recognized for years as one of the fine resort motels on the Oregon Coast, serves fine food that compliments the million-dollar vista of rocks and beach. **The Lounge & Loft** opens for lunch at noon; closes at midnight daily.

La Serre in the center of town is a refreshing, attractive eating place, featuring seafood, omelets, steaks and vegetarian menus—all excellent.

The Yachats Pie and Kite Shop is that "something special" place for lunches and breaks no one should miss. Tucked away on Ocean View Drive a block west of the highway, it really does combine pies (home baked by the owners) and kites (from around the world). Customers know the pies are out of the oven when they see a kite flying from the building.

Annual Events

An **Arts and Crafts Fair** in March offers an opportunity for visitors to view the works of many regional artists and craftspeople who live and work along the Oregon Coast.

Smelt Beach Park Wayside at Yachats borders the length of beach where netters come by the thousands each year to harvest the silver smelt with specially designed nets. This region is one of a few places in the world where the small fish come to mate. A community smelt fry—held annually to celebrate the smelt run—draws visitors from all over the West Coast.

The $75,000 cast bronze sculpture of a sea lion family, work of metal sculptor Ken Scott, installed in 1982 to commemorate the 50th anniversary of Sea Lion Caves. The life-sized work is placed near the head of the protected trail that descends to the elevators at the cavern entrance.

SEA LION CAVES

Entering Oregon's world famous **Sea Lion Caves** is like moving into another universe. The caves, ranked among the most impressive of the earth's famous caverns, are compared frequently—perhaps inevitably—with the magnificent Blue Grotto of Capri.

The chamber is awesome: two acres of smooth stone surfaces and rock projections under a dome rock ceiling 125 feet high; its walls softly striped in muted grays and greens and sand tones and pinkey-reds that mark off the ages, layer by layer, which comprised the earth's ancient surfaces along the present shoreline; subsequently carved by the relentless action of the sea, working over milleniums, to this splendid cavern at the base of the 325 foot headland.

The nucleus of the cave is the great rock centered in the ocean pool, surrounded by tiers of tumbled stones. It is here that the families of stellar sea lions live—as many as 600 during the winter, tapering off to a few dozen during the warmer months. These are the largest of the eared sea lions. Weighing around 50 pounds at birth, the bulls often grow to over a ton at maturity. The cows, much slenderer than the males, weigh up to 700 pounds each.

These huge mammals have teeth and feed on fish, sometimes descending 600 feet into the ocean depths in search of food. They can forage under water for periods of up to five minutes before coming up for air. The animals live in harems of 15 to 20 cows to a senior bull on the ledges outside the caves during the summer months, breeding and giving birth there. Because the cows desert the family structure easily, the herd bulls must maintain an around-the-clock alert against bachelor bulls eager to capture harems for themselves.

The animals are protected by law against killing or capture, and operators of the caves are careful to extend that protection to prevent disturbance by the thousands of visitors who come into the cave to observe them in their natural environment each year. Observation areas, while offering unobstructed views of the sea lions, are not close enough to upset the creatures. Signs caution visitors to speak softly; cameras are allowed, but only without flash units. Maintenance and improvements are handled at times when there is minimal chance of upsetting the herd.

The caves were discovered in 1880 by a Captain William Cox who later explored them by entering the cavern during calm weather in a small boat. Some years after the discovery he bought the land and the caves from the state, and it remained in his family's possession until 1927, when it was sold to a partnership for development as a tourist attraction.

A trail over a quarter of a mile long was constructed down the cliff face, ending in an enclosed wooden staircase that led to the northern entrance, and the caves were opened to the public in the fall of 1932. The steep trail and the long staircase, while not dangerous, were forbidding in stormy weather. An elevator, begun in 1959, was completed in mid-summer of 1961 at a cost of $180,000. Since that time the caves have been operated as a year-around enterprise, easily accessible to children and older persons, no longer restricted to adventurous parties willing to descend the outside path to watch the animals at sea level.

FLORENCE

Florence, named after a board that floated in to shore from the wreckage of a vessel of the same name, is the halfway point of the Oregon coast. The settlement at the mouth of the Siuslaw River was assured when one William Moody set up a store in an Indian shack and started a post office in 1876, the year the Siuslaw Valley was opened to settlers. Before that time the land had belonged to the Siuslaw tribe, but was gradually maneuvered away from them by treaties that as late as 1979 had not been honored by the United States government.

Florence Waterfront

A small **Gazebo** set in a landscaped area overlooking the river offers a shady spot for walkers and bikers to rest. A ramp nearby leads down to a dock where young and old come to sit and wait, rod in hand, for the fish to bite.

A walk colorful with plantings leads through a modern office complex and on to the historic **Mapleton Depot** moved a dozen miles downstream to its present site several years ago. The building now houses **Catch The Wind Kites**; this one, as in the branches located at Lincoln City and Newport, aflutter inside and out with irridescent kites like glittering butterflies.

Across the street from the gazebo is the historic **Kyle & Sons** commercial building, erected in 1905. A landmark in Florence, it is now occupied by **The Bridgewater** restaurant.

Several attractive shops are close together on the river side of the street. **Kitchen Klutter** is an unusual kitchen shop with a stock of attractive, practical gadgets you wouldn't believe: circular spice or salt shakers with six individually-lidded compartments, to be combined as recipes require by opening the required lids, for one. For two — a handy-dandy plastic pouch opener for access to the hermetically sealed packages that are all but impossible to open. For three: for specialty gift breads, shiny pans ranging from doll-sized (2x2½ inches) to jumbo. For four and for fun: ceramic cookie stamps with charming designs for making plain cookies elegant — owls and flowers and kittens and toys — there's even one with an umbrella and raindrops. And hanging on one wall, a collection of bloomer aprons, to wear over pants or jeans. This is the place to find remembrance gifts and "littles" for fun giving for those "under $5.00" occasions.

The Bay Window in the next block is a loverly, quiet place chock full of lovely leftovers from the past — chairs and jewelry and glass, gentlemen's pocket watches, old-fashioned straight-edge razors and such. And for those who can't resist vintage books and magazines and posters and placards and prints, it's a treasure house. New works of art hang in the gallery end along with stained glass. There's a pipe and tobacco section too. It's a shop steeped in serenity, and no one interrupts the serious browser unless asked for help. Don't pass this one by.

Nearby is **Incredible Edible Oregon** featuring foods and gifts produced in the state, including a selection of Oregon wines (and handsome hand-printed bottle sacks for gift-wrapping same). "Home grown" items here include toys and novelties as well as foods; and a good selection of books by Oregon authors.

The Stuffed Cubbyhole has one of the best collections of hand needlework and fine sewing on the Oregon coast, not only for exquisite workmanship but for superior design as well. Designer dresses — toddlers to twelves — are beautifully crafted of fine cottons. Hangings and dolls and gift items are displayed to show each at its best.

Interesting Sights and Sites

From the outside **The Toy Factory** in a plain gray building doesn't appear to be a time-travel machine that transports adult visitors back into childhood with none of the startling side effects felt during takeoff in a 747 jet. But stepping through the door, both new parents and senior citizens may find themselves acting like play schoolers.

Another such variety of original playthings will not be found south of Santa's workshop! There's something special about every toy in the shop. Puppets aren't just animated gloves; stuffed fur skunks and raccoons come alive on small hands slipped inside these three-dimensional animals.

Wood toys are much in evidence: trains and planes and cars and stick horses, tractors and trucks (one with a carload of dominoes) line the shelves in lengths ranging from two inches to two feet. Imported, hand-crafted wood carnival toys — a ferris wheel, an airplane swing, a carousel — are potential collectors' items. Jigsaw puzzles for younger children are made of polished wood: custom designs feature the letters of a child's name that fit into cutout spaces on a panel faced with backing to keep them from falling through. A more elaborate sampler board has a cutout alphabet, numbers one to zero, and sliding counting beads. The Alpha Bag is a bag full of wooden letters, each individually cut and polished from pine. Extra letters can be ordered.

Among their original toy designs is a marble juggler — a series of slanted chutes challenges the player to see how many marbles can be kept in motion by catching each as it comes to the bottom of the board and dropping it into the top, keeping several in the chutes at once. Easy? Well, the rules specify *one hand only*. They supplement their own unusual toys with those made by craftspersons and small businesses, all of superior quality. The shop also includes a fine selection of books for children.

The Toy Factory is located about five miles north of Florence on the highway. Anyone passing by is invited to stop in and play for awhile.

The Indian Forest, as one might suspect, is a collection of replicas of authentic Indian dwellings set up in the forest four miles north of Florence. Forest paths lead through huckleberries and rhododendrons past full-sized reproductions of various types of Indian shelters: earth-mound lodge, plank long house, birch bark lodge, and others, in addition to the familiar plain tipi. The complex also includes a small herd of buffalo.

The Indian Trading Post at the entrance carries a wide selection of handmade Indian art: Navajo rugs and jewelry, Zuni beadwork, Hopi pottery, Kachinas, sand paintings, baskets and moccasins. Souvenir-type items include hand-braided leather whips, "coonskin" caps, toys and such.

Travelers will recognize the Indian Forest by the giant colored totem pole in front. The forest is open May through October.

An unusual nature study exhibit is the **Darlingtonia Wayside** located nearby on the opposite side of the highway. These exotic *Darlingtonia* plants, popularly known as cobra lilies, are carnivorous, trapping and eating insects as part of the life support system. Normally found in large bogs each side of the Oregon/California border, this particular area has been designated as a botannical preserve to allow interested persons to observe the large fields close up. Raised walkways in keeping with the natural environment are built through the fields of giant plants rearing their hooded leaves high from the root base, for all the world like a nest of the snakes which have given them their common name. Restrooms and a few picnic tables are part of the small wayside park, just off the highway on a paved street, with well-placed directional signs.

Woodsman's Native Nursery deals in plants and trees that grow naturally in the coastal area. For over 15 years it has been supplying such native products as huckleberry, salal, ferns, caenothus, manzanita, Oregon grape, Port Orford cedar, Scotch broom to other nurseries around the country.

Another specialty of the house is wild berry jams and jellies — huckleberry, blackberry, blueberry and salal — homemade in the immaculate kitchen which is part of the modern building housing the garden shop. Each year hundreds of gallons of juice are processed and frozen while the berries are in season and made up in small batches as orders come in. And they come from all over the world. Gift packs including one jar of each flavor are postpaid in the continental USA.

Dolly Wares Doll Museum just north of Florence has been around for quite a while. The collection of more than 2,500 dolls, many of them dressed in their original costumes, is impressive. The oldest dates back to pre-Columbian times — a four-inch clay figure. Some wooden dolls go back to the 17th Century. They are of all types and sizes: china and metal and celluloid dolls, wax and papier mache dolls, baby dolls and mama dolls and kewpies and Barbies — you name it, it's probably here. The largest is six feet tall. The smallest —? Some dressed fleas —

Where do the dolls come from? Some are donated, others are purchased. Some are collected piece by piece and assembled at the museum. It is the only repair and restoration facility for dolls in this part of the state, which is patronized by a large number of out-of-state clients. Replacing glass eyes is the most difficult part of the restoration process. The best ones come from East Germany and are hard to get now.

Doll collecting has grown in the last ten years until it is crowding for number one as a "collector" activity. Reproductions of former doll favorites such as the Kewpie dolls of the 1920's is another current trend. The Museum has the original Skippy doll from which the molds were made for modern reproductions of the once favorite toy.

Dolly Wares is a fascinating place for adults and children alike — and children must be accompanied by an adult. But the charge is reasonable and cameras (without flash or tripod) are allowed in the well-lighted display hall.

Coastal Mountain Stables adds a new dimension to coastal exploration — horseback riding. Whether riding through the surf at sundown or following a mountain trail to get an overview of beach and ocean, riders can view the spectacular ocean beaches north of Florence from a new perspective. There are pony rides, too, for smaller children; and something from the past for young and old to enjoy — hay rides. Located 8 miles north of Florence on Highway 101, C & M Stables are open 7 days a week summers; 6 days a week November 15-March 15 (closed Tuesdays).

Fine Foods in Florence

Long-time vacationers in the Florence area remember the **Windward Inn**'s beginnings as a lunch counter and a gas station in the mid-1930's. It has evolved through a series of renovations to its present eminence as one of the finest restaurants not only on the Oregon coast, but in the state.

Van and Kathie Heeter, owners of the Windward Inn, welcome guests "as a friend would welcome them into their homes." Stepping into the quiet charm of the Inn's dining areas, furnished with comfortable antiques in keeping with its "American Renovation" architectural style, diners can relax over excellent meals served with care.

The Windward Inn's menu is comprehensive to satisfy the tastes of almost anyone. The *Accompaniments* list includes both French fries and fresh sauteed mushrooms; you can order a luncheon of homemade pate, toasted bagel, fresh fruit and soup, or a hamburger; a pocket sandwich of chicken breasts and avocado, or a hot dinner sandwich. And they'll all have one thing in common: each will be excellent in its own way.

But it is the "littles" added to the excellent food that makes this the very special place it is. This is a FAMILY dinner house, and children are welcome. Special smaller servings for juniors and seniors solve a real problem for those who can't eat large servings and dislike wasting good food.

Excellence is really the definitive word in describing the Windward Inn. Desserts and pastry are homemade every day; each pot of coffee is ground fresh; mussels are gathered daily by the staff from local beaches in season for their Sea Mussels Mariniers. A fine selection of wines is offered plus cocktail service during the dinner hour.

New recipes or seasonal foods are featured as daily specials. A traditional Merchant's lunch is different every day. They will gladly accommodate special dietary requests. *Gladly* makes the difference.

The new **Mo's** on the Florence docks at the site of the one that burned has wrap-around window walls on three sides instead of the tiny porthole windows of the earlier one. But fishnets drape the beams in this new cannery-type setting, and tables and benches are the order of the day, although brighter and glossier than the ones in the old building. The same excellent chowder and garlic bread are served here as before, although prices seem to have inched up a bit. But it's still a great place to rest and eat and watch the river. You really can't go wrong stopping for a meal at a **Mo's**.

Weber's Fish Market and Restaurant serves good seafood at good prices; or stop at the market side and choose fresh fish to prepare at home.

Fisherman's Wharf in Old Town specializes in hearty food to appease the appetites of fishermen and loggers. Breakfasts, served all day, are generous, featuring hotcakes the size of dinner plates, healthy portions of hash browns, and very good coffee.

The annual **Rhododendron Festival** at Florence has an edge on other coast celebrations — about 73 years. But even after more than three-quarters of a century of putting on the event each spring when the Rhodies bloom, it's still growing and improving.

You'd think after all that time there wouldn't be anything new in the way of activities to try, but each year finds some changes in the calendar of entertainment to attract the thousands of visitors who throng the town during the festivities.

Since the first festival in 1908, Florence has elected a festival queen and staged a parade every year except for during World War I.

Annual Events

Boat Show — March
The Rhododendron Festival — May
Fourth of July Celebration — July
Hard Times Carnival — October
Christmas Parade and Party — December

Notes:

Up front **The Sand Dunes Frontier** appears to be one more attractive tourist enterprise offering a variety of fun activities: their advertising uses the old familiar adjectives tourists see and hear *ad infinitum*: "most beautiful," "outstanding," "the world's tallest, or first, or smallest —"

Private fishing ponds and mini golf courses like the ones found here are not unique along the coast; and gift shops abound. But Sand Dunes Frontier has the first and best dune buggy game going, and that's what makes it special

This is a friendly place. The driver jokes as he helps passengers — from tots to seniors — into his vehicle; and they make their own jokes as they choose their seats and fasten their seat belts. But the moment the buggy enters the world of towering sand hills, silent except for the subdued growling of the engine as the vehicle follows shadow tracks along the contoured ridges, the riders become silent too.

The effect for passengers is a little like taking a whirl on a 200-acre roller coaster. The driver stops frequently to allow riders to catch their breaths and take photographs. Small fresh water lakes are tucked away like emeralds in the folds at the bottoms of the steep valleys. From the high crests they appear as bonsai dish gardens, fringed by dark green conifers limned against rich sand tones with the spare perfection of oriental brush paintings. Water in the lakes, 20 feet deep in some, stays fresh and good for drinking. They make excellent swimming holes on warm days. Air currents keep them from filling in, although the contours of the dunes themselves shift endlessly.

The golden sand billows as far as the eye can see — 32,000 acres of it — (60,000 if you count the 35-mile stretch which underlaps the ocean along the shore line) centered here by the world's highest sand dune. At just under 400 feet it is taller than any in the Sahara. It is here the National Dune Buggy Association regional competitions are held annually, when as many as a hundred of the dune "bugs" wallow and grind through their paces on the massive sand mound.

More than 75,000 people, both tourists and groups, take the dunes rides annually. This is a year-around activity, weather permitting, although 80 percent of the clients come in July and August. Buggies carry up to 20 people; more if children are held. There is no charge for youngsters under five who sit on parents' laps.

So — the neat 18-hold miniature golf course is popular with tourists. And children place the trout lake, where they can fish for a sure catch, high on their lists. The gift shop offers fine imports along with souvenir items. But it is the unique experience of entering the majestic sand dune wilderness that keeps visitors returning; and they come from all over the world. This is a good family stop; one not to be bypassed. Watch for the sign just past Honeyman Park south of Florence on Highway 101.

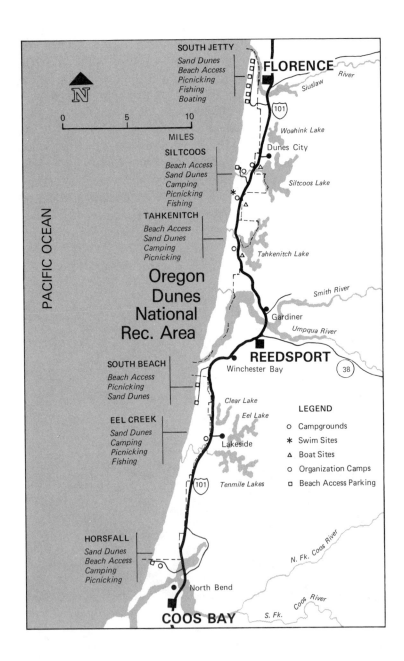

SOUTH JETTY
Sand Dunes
Beach Access
Picnicking
Fishing
Boating

FLORENCE

Siuslaw River

101

Woahink Lake

Dunes City

SILTCOOS
Beach Access
Sand Dunes
Camping
Picnicking
Fishing

Siltcoos Lake

TAHKENITCH
Beach Access
Sand Dunes
Camping
Picnicking

Tahkenitch Lake

0   5   10
MILES

N

PACIFIC OCEAN

Oregon
Dunes
National
Rec. Area

Smith River

Gardiner

Umpqua River

REEDSPORT

SOUTH BEACH
Beach Access
Picnicking
Sand Dunes

Winchester Bay

38

Clear Lake

Eel Lake

EEL CREEK
Sand Dunes
Camping
Picnicking
Fishing

Lakeside

LEGEND

o   Campgrounds
✳   Swim Sites
△   Boat Sites
o   Organization Camps
▢   Beach Access Parking

101   *Tenmile Lakes*

HORSFALL
Sand Dunes
Beach Access
Camping
Picnicking

N. Fk. Coos River

North Bend

Coos River

COOS BAY   *S. Fk.*

GARDINER

Gardiner — The White City by the Sea — was established by crewmen of the shipwrecked *Bostonian* in October of 1850, the year the Territorial Legislature established 5,000 square miles of southern Oregon land between Roseburg and the coast as Umpqua County.

The *Bostonian* was one of three ships sent by San Francisco developers which were carrying supplies to expedite settlement of four new cities along the Umpqua River, the largest between the Columbia and San Francisco Bay. The developers, anticipating this would be the Northwest's shortest route to the gold fields of California, planned to establish Myrtle Grove at the head of tidewater (now Scottsburg), Elkton near the site of the Hudson Bay Company's Fort Umpqua, Winchester on the Oregon-California Trail, and Umpqua City at the mouth of the harbor.

Most of the cargo from the wrecked ship was salvaged and carried nine miles north, and Gardiner's first buildings were erected. The town was named for the man who had piloted the *Bostonian* around Cape Horn. But it was W. J. Jewett, manager of the town's lumber mill — then as now its major business — who persuaded homeowners to paint their residences white, as those of his hometown in New England had been. Eventually every building in the community was so painted. Even today most are white, including the antique church with its bright red door on the bluff overlooking the town — the oldest mission still operating on the coast. A few newer houses along the highway at the edge of town flaunt bold colors, but they are few.

From the time it was built until the railroads came to the area in 1916, Gardiner was the industrial and cultural core of the region.

Terraced levels of a pioneer cemetery bank the hill across from
the sprawling mill buildings which dominate the town. The
elaborate headstones, moss-covered now inside the burial
plots fenced with ornamental railings, bear dates in the early
1860's.

REEDSPORT/WINCHESTER BAY

Reedsport has been fighting a battle since its founding to keep its feet dry. The marshy ground on which it is built was flooded as often as not, and the original buildings and walkways were on stilts, as much as eight feet above ground level, to prevent their flooding. Later the ground was filled in, and in the mid-1950's a dike was built to protect the town from the water.

Sister city **Winchester Bay** is four miles southwest of Reedsport, but a road between the two was not completed until 1926. Together they form an entity which is the nucleus of the most popular sport fishing area on the coast. Reedsport is the general business area for the region as evidenced by the buildings flanking the highway through town.

Posey's Bakery and Cafe in a shopping complex on the highway near the center of town is a lunch stop worth noting: above average menu items in an informal setting, with a case full of mouth-watering pastries for take-alongs.

A few old buildings remain in the Reedsport's old town section; notable is the **Reedsport Cheese Shoppe**. Although cheddar cheese is no longer produced in the former plant, they concoct natural whole milk flavored cheeses from a cheese base purchased from nearby cheese factories. In the spring the old brick building, painted white and fronted with a pink-and-white striped awning, looks rather like a gift package, with two giant rhododendrons in flower masquerading as pink bows. Appropriately, for gourmet gift food items produced in the region are also carried here, including cranberry sweets, wild berry jams, and goat milk shaving soap. The shop is easy to spot on Oregon highway 38, a half mile east of Highway 101.

Some interesting, and excellent, food choices are offered at the **Harbor Light Restaurant** at the south end of the bridge. The driftwood gray exterior of the building suits its locale. Owner G.A. Serang grew up on India's southern coast, and brings a unique Indian accent to the rich varieties of seafood found in the Reedsport area. The menu features more than a dozen original-recipe entrees adapted to American tastes (an approach Serang has expanded at the **International Burger and Seafood** in Waldport, where the menu features food flavors from eight countries). Prices: reasonable. Servings: generous.

Across the highway is the headquarters for the **Oregon Dunes National Recreation Area**, 40 miles long with a width varying from one to two-and-a-half miles. That's a 32,400 acre playground dedicated to public use and enjoyment, with added attractions not usually found in "dune country" — lakes and rivers and forests and wildlife. One of the largest such areas in the world, it is administered by the US Forest Service. The office, open weekdays, is an informational gold mine for vacationers and tourists to the dunes area.

Winchester Bay, the recreational center, was named for one of the original San Francisco developers of the Umpqua region in 1850. The seemingly quiet little harbor village located there generates a lot of fun activitiy which, along with excellent fishing, draws thousands of visitors to the area each year.

A new **US Coast Guard** facility has spruced up the north end of the Salmon Harbor area, with stations for rescue vessels and maintenance around the office quarters. Visitors are welcomed here but are asked to check in at the front office upon arrival to arrange for a conducted tour.

Several charter services operate out of the harbor: **Shamrock Charters**, largest and oldest; the **Becky Lynn, Marsadon, Thompson Charter**, and **Holiday**; plus a boat launching facility, **The Salmon Harbor Boat Lift. The Sportsmans Cannery** will process a day's catch for later pickup, or exchange already canned products on the spot. They also market processed and fresh seafood, and will ship gift packs for customers. Fresh ocean products are also available at area markets in variety — **Bayside Seafood** and **Dick's Seafood** for instance.

Showcase installation is **Salmon Harbor** marina, the largest (and without question one of the most attractive) sport fishing facilities on the Oregon coast. There are 925 moorings in the harbor, about a third of them used by commercial boats. Operated jointly by Douglas County and the Port of Umpqua, Salmon Harbor is self-supporting. Fees for moorage are figured at $10 a foot per year. Monthly fees too are based on boat size. Several hundred overnight camping spaces for self-contained RV's rent at $4/night. Information is available at the modern office building at the entrance.

Across from the marina, **Windy Cove Campground** is operated by Douglas County. Protected by a hill, with lawns and trees and hookups, it is ideal for family vacations. Amenities include a store, a playground, and a location within walking distance of dunes and beaches.

Surfwood Campground and RV Park located half a mile north of Winchester Bay has 140 sites with water, electricity, and some hook-ups. Additional conveniences include a fish cleaning area, showers, sauna, dump station, and store; plus tennis, horseshoe, and shuffleboard courts and a heated pool. Play equipment signout is offered without charge.

This is preferred territory for Chinook and silver salmon, found in Ocean and river alike. Steelhead are plentiful in both the Smith River and the Umpqua — the largest river flowing into the Pacific between the Columbia and San Francisco. The rivers also yield sturgeon, perch, shad, and Dungeness crab. Nearby lakes are noted for fine rainbow trout, crappie, and bluegills. The area is truly a fisherman's paradise in terms of variety and abundance.

But to chronicle a whopping good fish tale is not to say it all! There are some super specials for those who wait patiently for the fishing enthusiasts to return with their bounty from the sea.

For openers, browsers will find one of the outstanding gift and art galleries on the Oregon coast. **Captain Bly's** is quality all the way. Here you will find oils and watercolors and scrimshaws by artist Don McMichael; incomparable metal sculpture by Ken Scott — a dimensional Spanish galleon in full sail, three feet long and three feet high, for instance; photography and weavings and stained glass; handmade dolls, including Amish dolls made without faces to avoid violating the biblical injunction against making "graven images"; and Christmas ornaments *extraordinaire*: sand dollars dipped in 24 karat gold, porcelain angel heads by Paula Meyer, hand-blown glass butterflies and birds and unicorns. There's always a bowl of salt water taffy on the counter for visitors to help themselves. This is an easy, friendly place to visit, and hardly anyone comes by who doesn't see something *just right* for a hard-to-buy-for friend, or spy a special hard-to-find personal gift.

Every coastal community worth its salt has a "you can't leave town without stopping" eatery, and Winchester Bay is no exception. Those who don't enjoy a breakfast/lunch/coffee break stop at **The Seven Seas** have only themselves to blame. (The emphasis is on *enjoy*.) Marilyn and Jim Flemming have spent more than 20 years keeping this a small, convivial, fun cafe where anyone who walks through the door is welcomed as an old friend. The walls are filled floor-to-ceiling with photographs and cards and mementos presented by habitues as thanks for the special combination of good food and good company. Their motto, No. 6 on their published house rules, establishes the fun level: "Good food takes time to prepare, yours will be ready in a second."

Before leaving, walk or drive to the top of the hill for a close-up of the **Umpqua River Lighthouse**, historic tower that houses the only signal light flashing a red beam on the Oregon coast. The former keeper's house is now a historical museum.

A group of houseboats cluster near the bridge over the Ump-qua River at Reedsport, complete with television antennas and clotheslines. The water-borne homes recall earlier days when the central town of Reedsport was built on stilts as much as eight feet above the ground to keep buildings from flooding.

It's easy to become addicted to Winchester Bay. Lodging is plentiful and central: **The Harbor View Motel**, neat and pleasant, at prices you won't believe; and the **Winchester Bay Motel**, larger, with a penthouse suite for a superb ocean view; and both a few steps away from the bay. In fact, everything in Winchester Bay is within walking distance of everything else.

If life in the lazy lane begins to appeal as retirement age nears, fine accommodations for permanent "vacation living" are available at **Pacific Sands Hometel** just north of Winchester Bay on Highway 101. The new facility offers studio, one and two bedroom apartments; three home-cooked meals a day, maid service, no charge laundry center; mini-bus transportation for necessary appointments, shopping and activities; utilities, telephone and cable TV on a monthly rental basis.

Annual Events

Fleet Days Ocean Fest the last weekend in July features a parade, teen dance, an Arts & Crafts show, and a rescue demonstration by the Coast Guard.

Notes:

Lacy steel scallops hang between concrete supports of the Yaquina Bay Bridge which spans the bay at Newport (above). The bridge and the Siuslaw Bridge (below) are two of the set of five coastal bridges completed during the 1930's depression under the Works Progress Administration (WPA).

The Bridges

A series of graceful bridges spans the major bays and rivers along the Oregon coast highway. The highway itself, begun in 1921, was conceived as a motor road following the coastline to be called the Roosevelt Military Highway. Prior to its construction sections of the beach served as roadways for vehicle travel and were passable only at low tide. It was completed in 1932.

Prime promoter of the project was Benjamin F. Jones, founder of the small community of Otter Rock north of Newport. He purchased the area for the site from one of the holders of a land allotment issued as replacement for tribal lands taken over by the government during the 1880's.

The concrete bridge across Rocky Creek near Whale Cove is named for Jones, "the father of the Oregon coast highway." The high, narrow arches anchor the span in a deep ravine visible from Otter Crest loop along a section known as "Ben's own wagon road" before it was incorporated into the highway constructed in the 1920's.

In January of 1934 $5,103,000 was designated for the construction of five coast bridges by the Works Progress Administration, the agency set up to create federal jobs during the 1930's depression by Franklin Delano Roosevelt. The five arched bridges were the final links in a hundred miles of central coast highway which opened the entire coastline as a major recreational and retirement area, easily accessible from inland valleys and neighboring states.

The **Yaquina Bay Bridge** at Newport was completed in 1936. The spans of the cantilevered bridge seem to tiptoe delicately across the bay, the large central deck arching almost 140 feet above the water to allow entrance of ocean-going freighters into the port area.

Waldport's **Alsea Bay Bridge** is a three-span cantilevered bridge, with a clearance of 70 feet, which carries traffic over the bay at the mouth of the Alsea River.

At Florence the **Siuslaw River Bridge**, the central one in the series, marches sturdily across the mouth of the Siuslaw River, supported by four thick concrete columns. These stolid underpinnings capped by dome headings resemble a quartet of medieval guardhouses from a distance.

The **Umpqua River Bridge** crosses the Umpqua River near Gardiner, close to its junction with Smith River, named for Mountain Man Jedediah Smith. The bridge is similar in design to its sister bridges—graceful steel spans on either side of a cantilevered archway.

McCullough Bridge at North Bend is the fifth WPA bridge. It is the longest—almost a mile—and the most expensive, with three suspension arches over the main channel supported on either side by a smaller concrete span. The channel spans clear 150 feet to accommodate ocean-going vessels. It is named for the designer of the bridges, C. B. McCullough, veteran bridge builder, and was dedicated June 5, 1936.

In an era when public sound equipment was just appearing on the American scene, some of the bridges were served at their dedications by one of the three Standard Oil Sound Trucks, which operated up and down the West Coast out of San Francisco at public gatherings for several years, in the same manner as the Goodyear blimps which for decades have floated above the crowds at public ceremonies around the country.

The **Isaac L. Patterson Bridge**, which crosses the Rogue River at Gold Beach, is named for the man who was Oregon's Governor from 1926 to 1929.

Thomas Creek Bridge north of Gold Beach is the highest bridge in Oregon. Rising 350 feet above ground level, it is higher than the Golden Gate Bridge—one of the world's longest bridges—with a span of less than a thousand feet.

Newest of Oregon's coastal bridges is the Astoria toll bridge, which crosses the Columbia River between that city and Megler, Washington—the world's longest continuous truss bridge, and the 16th in overall length (21,697 feet). Until the completion of the bridge in 1966, crossings were made by ferry.

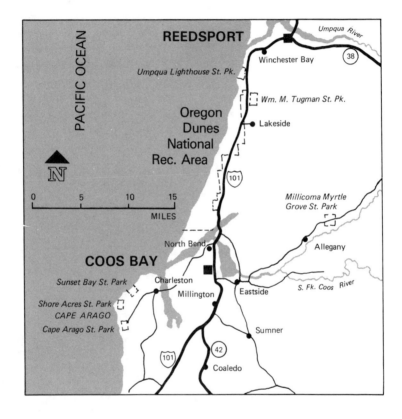

North Bend
Coos Bay
Charleston

NORTH BEND

Coos Bay/North Bend is the world's largest shipping point for timber products. The first lumber was exported from the area in 1846, and two years later the brig *Blanco* came off the ways, the first ship built at the Simpson shipyards in North Bend.

The City of Coos Bay was originally named Marshfield by its founder, who raised the first structure there in 1854. It was incorporated as a city twenty years later; in 1944 the name was officially changed to Coos Bay.

North Bend, two miles to the north, was settled in 1853 and acquired by Asa Simpson in 1856, to become a company owned town for Simpson mill and shipyard employees. In 1903 Louis Simpson, son of the founder, was instrumental in incorporating the city.

Interesting Things to See and Do

The Coos-Curry Museum in North Bend is a treasure chest of area history. But displays in the modern building in Simpson Park at the south end of the McCullough Bridge offer far more than antique furnishings and equipment. The usual array of furniture and china and tools and ornaments from an earlier day are preserved and presented there — among them a turn-of-the-century Regina Music Box, a handmade spinning wheel, and the customary fine piano which had been shipped around Cape Horn.

But there is more.

Relics of the coastal area are represented by maritime artifacts such as the steering wheel from the *Roosevelt*, one of the freighters produced in the Simpson shipyards, which operated regularly between North Bend and Glasgow, Oregon for years. Also on display is an outstanding collection of eighteen boat models handcrafted of inlaid wood by boat designer Frank Lowe, a joy to see and touch.

A delicate Chinese plaque inlaid with red, white, green and bronze jade on black lacquer which floated ashore from the freighter *Brush* when it broke up on Simpson reef during a winter storm is especially lovely.

A comprehensive selection of Indian artifacts fills a section. Notable are aprons of intricate beadwork, one trimmed with small shells, the other decorated with sixty-five brass thimbles like a fringe of bells. Beadwork ceremonial robes are colorful and beautifully detailed. Baskets in an assortment of sizes and shapes, from two inches to two bushels, fill another corner. A stubby totem pole stands guard at a doorway near a fine collection of arrowheads said to be one of the best on the coast.

One unusual collection contains fifty-nine slingshots, each one shaped by a local carver from a different native northwest wood. And in a special corner, seashore art of natural shells and driftwood is displayed in scenes which appear to be an arrangement of hand-carved human and animal figures. An antique wooden leg supplies a humorous touch.

Exhibits of antique logging equipment are on display in Simpson Park adjacent to the Coos-Curry Museum, including the steam boiler shown here. The Museum is located at the south end of McCullough Bridge in North Bend. Collections include 59 hand-carved slingshots, each from a different native wood, and Indian beadwork.

Before leaving the museum grounds, visitors will want to investigate an old-time steam locomotive and other old logging equipment in the park nearby.

The museum is open every day except Monday. Hours May through September are 11:00 am to 5:00 pm. During the winter months the museum is open afternoons only.

Another historic building is **The Marshfield Sun Printing Museum** maintained as it was when it printed the newspaper for which it is named. It is open three afternoons a week during the summer months.

Pony Village

North Bend is the home for the southwest coast's largest shopping center, **The Pony Village Mall**, which provides a variety of businesses the average shopper would expect to find under one roof. The Mall, adjacent to the **Pony Village Lodge** also features a continuing program of exhibits and community events.

Cone 9 is a kitchen shop worth looking into. Watch for the unusual brick and timber facade while strolling the mall. Inside are some unusual gourmet cooking items — copper and pottery and wood and china, etc. They carry a good assortment of pasta equipment: ravioli pans and cutting machines adjustable to several widths; and an excellent selection of iron cookware — corn stick pans, egg poachers, oversized dutch ovens and such in addition to skillets of all sizes. It's a good place to find original kitchen gifts as well as quality basics.

Nature's Wooden Image gleams with reflections from copper, glass, and brass, as well as the sheen of myrtlewood. Wares in this gift shop are displayed with style, as befits the works of fine regional artists represented here. The carvings of master woodcarver R.D. Lewis capture the attention, whether carousel horses or decoys or cigar store Indians. Knot Heads — carvings of heads created from wood knots by Pete Wills, so lifelike in appearance one almost expects them to speak — hang near paintings and plates and whales created by Don McMichaels. Carved cedar whales, painted and barnacled, are so natural in appearance they could be alive. The shop projects an air of quality, an atmosphere enhanced by friendly service. Truly, the selections of gift and art pieces to be seen here is outstanding.

The large, well-lighted **House of Books** has what surely must be the longest magazine stand in the Northwest — one lengthy wall is covered with racks holding hundreds of the latest issues of periodicals, in addition to stacks and shelves of books. It's a bookworm's paradise if ever there was one.

This is a full-service mall, complete with clothing stores, shoe shops, candy shops, drink stands, and eateries. (And if the parisian sidewalk cafe area with white iron tables and chairs seem incongruous in this coastal mall, not to fret: there is a seafood grotto near the main entrance.)

COOS BAY

Coos Bay curves around the west side of the Bay for which it is named: a port town of 15,000 that displays traces of international influence due to foreign ships that regularly enter the Bay to load lumber products from the area. The flavor of the town is influenced too by the presence of Southwest Oregon Community College, which supports and enhances a traditional area interest in music and drama.

The **On Broadway Theatre** in Coos Bay started as a showcase for local talent via vaudeville-style theater alternating with the showing of film classics. It now presents year-around live theatre; as does **The Little Theater On The Bay**, Virginia and Washington, in North Bend. Across the street from the On Broadway, the 60-year-old **Egyptian Theatre** — complete with pipe organ and the extravagantly ornate Egyptian decor popular at the time it was built — is still showing movies.

And yet another **MO's**, this one sharing an atrium setting with a number of interesting shops in **The Golden Storehouse**. You can't miss it driving through town.

CHARLESTON

The **Charleston Small Boat Basin**, nine miles west of downtown Coos Bay, lies just inside what experts describe as "the safest bar on the Oregon Coast." Deep sea fishing is excellent. **Charleston Charters** and **B&B Charters** operate out of the harbor on a daily schedule. Tackle is furnished for both salmon and bottom fishing. Necessary licenses are available at the charger offices; nearby cafes pack fishermen's lunches; dock area canneries will freeze, smoke or can catches for transportation home. Reservations are required.

Three State Parks

An intermeshing system of state parks near Charleston provides one of the most attractive combinations of facilities and recreational activities anywhere on the coast. Among them they offer excellent camping, picnicking, and accommodations surrounded by scenic and outdoor fun areas unique in number and interest. And, except for the modest charges at overnight camping spots, all are available without charge. This is a fine location for a summer vacation in the old tradition of settling down for a week or two to enjoy the serenity and beauty of lazy days by the ocean.

Sunset Bay State Park is just that — a parkland providing both tent and trailer facilities in sheltered spaces which allow plenty of privacy. Excellent utility buildings are clean and convenient, with both laundry and shower accommodations for campers. Water and firewood are standard here.

Large covered shelters house electric stoves and other conveniences for group cookouts, with picnic tables close by. Cleaning tables are located in central areas for easy handling of the abundant catches anglers enjoy here. **Sunset Bay Golf**

Oriental gardens surround a sunken pool, centered by bronze herons, at the south end of four acres of formal landscaping which once embraced the mansion at Shore Acres, the elegant estate of West Coast shipping magnate Lewis J. Simpson. The gardens contain plantings from around the world, many brought from far countries in the sailing ships manufactured in the Simpson shipyards at North Bend. The gardens are maintained as a part of the state park system.

Course is part of the park system. The jewel-like Sunset Beach deserves its world-wide reputation for charm and beauty. It is sheltered by cliffs which are broken just enough to form a narrow sea channel, making it one of the calmest of the coast beaches.

Shore Acres, a short way up the road, looks like the setting for an episode of the old *Bonanza* TV series. Its story reads like one. Embracing 1,000 acres of wildly beautiful Oregon coastline, this is the site of the coastal empire developed by California shipping magnate Louis J. Simpson during the first half of the century.

Bounded on the north by South Bay, a delightfully secluded cove beach, the forested acres rise dramatically to the grandeur of Cape Arago, the headland which shelters the small harbor where Sir Francis Drake may have made his only landing during his exploration along the north Pacific coastline. The heart of the holdings, where the Simpson mansion once sat among acres of formal gardens, is guarded by monolithic cliffs carved by tides which send lashings of spray over the top of the seventy-five-foot promontory when coastal gales are blowing.

Simpson's father, Asa, came to California in 1849 to bring supplies to miners during the gold rush. Within ten years he had acquired timber holdings along the Pacific Coast north of San Francisco, establishing shipyards at Coos Bay, Oregon, and Gray's Harbor, Washington, from which more than fifty ships were produced to sail the world's oceans. Beginning in 1859 with the two-masted brig *Blanco*, his output increased during the next twenty years to include regular manufacture of four-masted vessels. In 1888 the first five-masted ship produced on the Pacific Coast was built at the Coos Bay yards — the schooner *Louis*.

His other business enterprises included lumber mills, logger operations, a fleet of freighters, and a packet service which linked Portland and San Francisco with regular runs.

Louis Simpson came to Oregon in 1899 to manage his father's interests and began development of the town of North Bend. He bought the central 320 acres of the estate in 1905 for $4,000 from a white settler who had recently lost his Indian wife. Playing on the man's loneliness, he negotiated the deal and began clearing the land the next year. In 1907 construction was begun on the fabled mansion, the largest house in Oregon in its time. A Christmas present for his wife, the mansion was used as a summer home until 1914, when a seventy-five foot addition added a ground floor bath house with a 26 foot by 52 foot swimming pool, bedrooms on the second floor, and a full-length ballroom on the third.

In July of 1921 the house and contents, sadly underinsured, were destroyed by fire, a catastrophe which undermined the Simpson fortune beyond recovery. Simpson moved into a small house on the estate from which he conducted his business. In 1923, salvaging lumber from one of his own schooners wrecked on Simpson's Reef off Shore Acres, he began construction of a second home — a ranch house 225 feet long — to be built by a Swedish contractor from plans drawn by a local draftsman. More informal than the first, the seventeen-room house surrounded by its formal gardens served as the center of the coastal estate. A nearby cove provided a private beach with picnic tables and bath houses; to the south were located a smaller ranch house and barns for the manager in charge of the herd of Simpson cattle which grazed the headlands of Cape Arago.

In the early 1930's Simpson donated 135 acres of his land to the State of Oregon for Cape Arago State Park. Ten years later the Simpson fortune, all but gone, could no longer support the luxurious estate, and Louis Simpson sold the remaining 637 acres of his Shore Acres property to the State for $29,000. The residence became a clubhouse for members of the tank battalion stationed at Cape Arago during World War II.

By 1948 the maintenance of the property had become too costly for the State of Oregon to justify, and the mansion was razed, except for the dining room wing which was moved and now serves as the garden cottage. Three years later the carriage house was also demolished.

But the magnificent botanical gardens, with plantings brought from all over the world by the Simpson ships, are maintained as part of the Oregon State Park system. In spite of severe damage during the Columbus Day storm in 1962, the gardens today are open the year around for public enjoyment.

Winding walkways entice viewers into hidden dells, past the sunken oriental ponds rimmed with plantings ranging from azaleas to palm trees which frame sculptured bronze herons whose graceful shadows are mirrored in the still surface of the water. Unsuspected clearings could serve as fairy courtyards which undoubtedly harbor elves. One irresistable path scrambles along the cliff tops like a frisky tomboy to the topmost point of Cape Arago.

There is no charge for enjoying the magnificent vistas, the splendid gardens, the sense of freedom one feels while standing in the wind on the cliff searching out the horizon line where sea and sky merge. Picnic tables and benches are placed in sheltered spots. It is not unusual to come upon a wedding in progress against the background of azaleas and rhododendrons.

And it is easy to reach by turning off Highway 101 at Coos Bay to the Charleston Boat Basin, then following the coast road around past Sunset Beach as it rises to the entrance of the Shore Acres estate. Viewpoints offer glimpses of the Cape Arago Lighthouse and an overview of Simpson's Reef, one of the most dangerous points for Pacific Coast sea traffic along the Oregon coastline.

Shore Acres is not a place to visit in a hurry. This majestic coastal panorama created over the ages by the relentless action of winds and tides seems to reduce time measured by minutes and hours to its proper proportions in relation to history.

Cape Arago is an area of great sandstone cliffs which seem to lean out over the ocean which beats against their footings in relentless lashings.

Cape Arago is a place of wild beauty, evolved over fifty million years by tidal activity whittling away at the shoreline. The spectacular results are sculptured sandstone bluffs unlike any others along the coast. Waves crashing against these inverted cliff formations are churned to a frothy white which turns the ocean to whipped cream around the roots of the great walls.

The winds blow over the small grassy headland atop Cape Arago as if determined to sweep it clean of intruders who insist on visiting this unprotected area. But the wide-angle view offered from the promontory with its small historic monument includes a glimpse of the tiny cove which — who knows — may have once provided harbor for Drake's *Golden Hind*.

Leave by the Back Road

The **Seven Devils Road** is a beach loop drive which takes travelers through charming rural countryside between Charleston and Bandon. The paved road is narrow in places and winds through the forested hills between Highway 101 and the shore. The drive offers access to three of the best "rock combing" beaches to be found along the coast: **Whiskey Run**, **Merchant's**, and **Agate** beaches. Stones of brilliant colors are abundant on all three of the beaches, along with agates and jasper.

The road, ten miles or so in length, rejoins Highway 101 just before it crosses the Coquille River north of Bandon.

Annual Events

The North Bend Air Show — June.

The Bay Area Fun Festival coordinated with the **Prefontaine Memorial Classic**, the 10,000 meter run held each year to commemorate famed runner Steve Prefontaine — September.

Freighter standing by for loading at the docks in Coos Bay.

Notes:

Doug Wilson displays two black rockfish and a ling cod caught from a rocky shore along the Oregon coast near Depoe Bay with new lures.

Catching More Bottom Fish

Here in the Pacific Northwest and along the Oregon Coast, anglers have access to a great many bottom species from small perch and flatfishes to large rockfishes in the 20-pound class. Ling Cod attain weights in excess of 60 pounds. Pacific Halibut reach 200 pounds. Many species may be taken on gear ranging from ultra-light spinning gear to wire-line-rigged boat rods.

For years the glamorous (and tasty) salmon and steelhead trout have overshadowed the bottom fish along Oregon's coast, bays, and estuaries. But salmon and steelhead trout are migratory and seasonal. They are also more difficult to catch for most anglers.

Bottom fish offer an alternative fishing challenge. They are available at all seasons of the year, eagerly attack a variety of lures and bait, are sporty on the right tackle, and are absolutely delicious on the table. Despite the availability of bottom fish all along Oregon's coast and salt-water inlets and bays, many anglers lack the know-how to consistently catch bottom fish. Many bottom fish may be caught accidentally while searching for salmon. But, when these same fishermen use new techniques and specially designed lures, they can enjoy hours of great fishing pleasure and an appreciation of the sport that bottom fish can provide when taken on tackle matched to the fishing conditions and the types of fish taken.

Many bottom fish are still caught using herring and salmon-style hookups, primarily because most fishermen seek bottom fish the same way they mooch for salmon. But, a fantastic breakthrough in bottom fishing techniques has evolved from research. These techniques, new to Oregon coast

151

waters, use leadhead jigs and plastic worms. They will amaze even dedicated bottom fishermen who have been using standard bait or jigging techniques. Originally developed for freshwater bass fishing and refined from jigs with pork rind, the leadhead jigs and plastic worms provide an entirely new approach to shallow-water bottom fishing.

This method is so effective that it has been used extensively in Puget Sound by the National Marine Fisheries Game Fish Project and Washington State Fisheries to collect bottom fish for tagging studies. More recently the Seattle Aquarium has been using shallow-water fishing techniques with leadhead jigs and plastic worms to collect display fish.

Black Rockfish are frequently found in schools feeding on or near the surface. A light steelhead rod or bass casting rod with jigs will bring strikes so fast and furiously you'll be wondering why you've never found the fish like this before.

Fishing early in the morning we have run into schools of surface-feeding Blacks. With both of us casting, we stayed constantly hooked up to fish for 30 minutes before we wore out our wrists landing and releasing Blacks as fast as we could cast and land them.

The secret to our success was simple—knowledge of proper rockfish habitat and lures that yield the greatest efficiency in fishing results. While salmon are fast-moving fish that charge through baitfish, more rockfish tend to lie in wait and make a short dash to grab the unsuspecting prey. Black and Yellowtail Rockfish do feed on small herring; however, they and other rockfish ambush their prey from close range.

By concentrating on shallow-water fishing, we've found that we can easily catch whatever fish we want to for our table, have more fun doing it, and are frequently able to go fishing more often by taking shorter but very productive trips. Bottom fish can be close at hand if you study the shoreline.

In slinging ¼-ounce jigs and plastic worms from the rocky shoreline at Depoe Bay, we found that we could land hard-running Blue Rockfish, a fish often mistaken for Black Rockfish. We were using light spinning tackle and waiting for the waves to help us lift our fish up to the rock ledge where we could land them. We were hooking and landing the Blues and Ling Cod within 100 feet of US Highway 101, the main street of this small fishing community—famous for salmon and bottom fishing charters. The area offers many miles of shoreline fishing possibilities. If you are traveling to the coast and your schedule does not permit time to go fishing by private or charter boat, don't overlook the opportunities for shore fishing. When we spotted the section of the rocky shoreline which obviously was several feet deep right at the water's edge, we knew that we had a likely spot. We quickly confirmed it by hooking a fish on the second cast. Enough action followed in the next half hour to provide several fish dinners.

We've fished plastic worm-leadhead jig combinations from cartoppers, piers and jetties, shoreline, and in the open ocean all along the Oregon coast. Jigs and plastic worms outfish bait on shallow-water rockfishes at least 5 to 1. The secret seems to be the curly-tailed plastic worms! The undulating tail movement of the worm adds that ingredient that must spell FOOD in capital letters to the hungry rockfish waiting for his next morsel to swim along.

The best part about fishing with these jigs is—if you already own a medium-weight mooching or steelhead rod and reel capable of casting these light jigs or even your lightweight tackle used for trout fishing, you've got everything you need except the jigs—to catch more fish and have more fun.

Doug Wilson
Fred Vander Werff

Authors of
"New Techniques for Catching Bottom Fish"

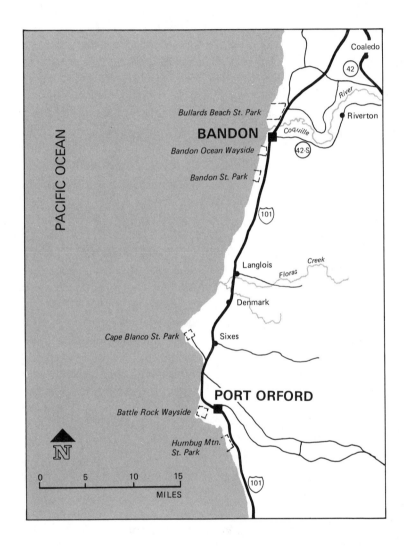

Coaledo

42

River

Riverton

Bullards Beach St. Park

BANDON

Coquille

42-S

Bandon Ocean Wayside

Bandon St. Park

PACIFIC OCEAN

101

Langlois

Creek

Floras

Denmark

Cape Blanco St. Park

Sixes

PORT ORFORD

Battle Rock Wayside

N

Humbug Mtn.
St. Park

101

| 0 | 5 | 10 | 15 |
MILES

Bandon
Port Orford

The beaches are studded with great rock formations, remnants of a historic coastline.

BANDON

Bandon, locale of famed **Face Rock** — the offshore natural sculpture carved by the battering tides — has a new face of its own. A renewal program begun in 1981 has transformed the once dilapidated **Old Town** into an area that begs to be explored. Sagging buildings dating back to the 30's, constructed hurriedly to replace those destroyed when a forest fire burned the town, have been rejuvenated; if not to youthful beauty, certainly to intriguing maturity.

Shops that once bordered the bayfront have relocated to new quarters in the "modern" Old Town. **Westerly Webs** weaving studio is a wonderland for weavers, knitters and macrame artists. Hanks of colored yarns spill from containers; hangings woven from hand-spun fibers show to perfection against display walls. Racks of hand woven, hand-knit vests, ponchos, and sweaters created by local craftspeople appeal to discriminating shoppers, bearing price tags far more moderate than the quality suggests; rugs and placemats and baskets are displayed creatively.

Spinning wheels and knitting machines of various sizes and complexities are available for buying or using. The owners, experts in their fields, offer individual instruction and hold classes for weavers and spinners who often come from other areas to participate. Special short-term classes are held during the summer to accommodate vacationers.

Others retain their long-time locations behind refurbished shop fronts that give them a new look. Across the street and down a short way **Whiskey Run Silver Shop** and **Bandon Art Glass Studio** share quarters resembling the inside of a treasure chest. The windows reflect light filtered through stained glass pieces; shelved walls and display cases sparkle and gleam from the hundreds of agates — polished or jeweled, carved or natural, mounted or not — found here.

Silversmith George Gaspar, who does his own lapidary work as well as the metalsmithing, combines semiprecious gems with silver and gold in truly imaginative forms to produce jewelry that is wearable as well as striking. A collection of picture jasper is interesting in larger pieces; smaller cuts made into rings and pendants are hauntingly lovely.

But it is the amazing array of agate and fossil forms that hold the limelight here. Delicate chalk-like fossils from the sea's depths ranging in size from tiny (an inch or even less) to a foot or more in height, formed with delicate precision, can be purchased for less than a dollar (the larger ones range up to $6) — the perfect souvenir from the Oregon coast in every sense of the word.

Next door is the **Bandon Card & Gift Shop** boasting the largest, most varied collection of greeting cards on the coast, wall-to-wall, literally; shelved on all sides, the center filled with turn-table racks. Clown cards, Betty Boops, Shirley Temple and Judy Garland repros; masks of movie greats with "nose holes" so the receiver can "become" Marilyn Monroe or Paul Newman for a time. There are even poison pen cards — red print on a black background with sarcastic sentiments inside.

But there is much more to this small shop than greeting cards. Unusual gifts are tucked away everywhere. Beautiful hand-crafted cut paper mobiles are exquisite in their delicacy: boat scenes, butterflies, birds, and flowers in dimensional design must be seen to be appreciated. Tiny French lithographs, matted and signed, under glass, add elegance to small table areas. "Unique" is an adjective much overworked in coastal descriptions but in this case it seems to be the only one that applies.

Charleston Pottery is shown in a big quiet room filled with casseroles and mugs (small to giant size), pitchers and tea pots and painted clay pigs, with lots of blue pieces among them. It is "unique" in its own manner — for there is no one minding this store. A sign directs interested customers to the work area where the distinctive pieces are produced. In a part of the state where pottery is as plentiful as beach sand, it isn't common to find pottery show rooms where individual items stand out, but here they do.

Some new enterprises have appeared among the familiar ones. The **230 Second Street Gallery** deserves its growing reputation as one of the outstanding galleries on the Pacific Coast. The superior handcrafts and excellent works of art exhibited here reflect the inherent beauty of the Bandon area, long a mecca for serious artists who find the natural environment a stimulus to the creative process.

Paintings, prints, sculpture, carvings, jewelry; glass and bronze and fiber; furnishings and accessories, each piece displayed with care to show to best advantage, enhances the overall attractiveness of the gallery. Professional artists staff the two-story exhibit area during visiting hours. And visitors are welcomed.

The **Continuum Center** is an unusual exhibit which combines research of science, religion, medicine, art, philosophy, psychology and parapsychology to explore the questions that have intrigued members of the human race since the beginning of time. An extensive library presents writings on metaphysical and occult subjects, pictures and graphics. Filmstrip presentation and demonstrations of kirlian photographs are part of the exhibit, originally shown at the California Museum of Science and Industry.

The Country Merchant looks like an old-fashioned country store, but it has an up-to-the-minute collection of gift and kitchen wares and toys. This is a friendly place — light and colorful and new-looking. And, impossible as it seems in a region bustling with gift stores, stocked with a variety of items not seen elsewhere.

A delightful piece is made of round hoops stretching net fabric filled with potpourri, ruffled and ringed for hanging as a room freshener, product of a local craftperson. Not hand-designed but eye-catching are canvas vegetable keepers, decorated with block print vegetable designs in bold colors; dampened, they keep vegetables fresh in the refrigerator for days. A rack near the counter holds old-fashioned hard candy drops in fresh-fruit flavors; cherry and lemon and orange and whatever, in old-fashioned candy sacks instead of plastic.

Down on the waterfront **Cranberry Sweets** is filled to overflowing with a delectable assortment of kitchen fresh candy of every variety and description: chocolates and caramels and nougats and fudge, by the piece or by the pound, packaged or choose your own; gift packages and containers too.

A visit to **Andrea's Old Town Cafe**, featuring "homemade food," is an experience not to be missed while in Bandon. The special recipes are prepared and served to the owner's choice for the day. Desserts are "melt-in-the-mouth" caliber. Allow time for a leisurely meal here; the servings are generous, the food is exceptional. Enjoy!

Another excellent choice for fine dining is **The Bandon Boatworks** at the end of the jetty road across from the abandoned lighthouse. A warm atmosphere adds to the enjoyment of superb food served without fanfare. At the top-notch salad bar, diners slice their own bread from homemade loaves. You'll find reasonable prices for fine cuisine here.

The Minute Cafe at the south end of Second Street opens for breakfast at 7:00 and serves dinner until 8:00 pm: "home cooking" that tastes like it: soups and pies and mashed potatoes made from scratch, with prices just as good.

The Three Gables up on the hill serves out-of-the-ordinary dinners and homemade desserts (not just pies, but cheese cake and Dutch Apple pie and such). Their generous children's menu offer makes it easy to take the family out to dinner.

Sea Star Hostel has dormitory style accommodations for 25, a kitchen area for use by guests, hot showers, a large public room with fireplace and piano for $7.50 for non-members of the American Youth Hostel organization; less for members. There are some restrictions: check-in time begins at 5:00 pm; checkout time is 10:00 am; guests do their own clean-ups. The youth reference in the title refers to the "young in heart," according to the manager. Sea Star is open the year around.

Cranberry Country

The major supply of the world's cranberries come from five US states: Massachusettes and New Jersey in the east, Wisconsin in the mid-west, and Oregon and Washington in the Pacific Northwest. Bandon is the cranberry capital of Oregon, with roughly 900 acres of this native American fruit in cultivation in Bandon area bogs.

The berries demand an acid peat base soil, and as a result are confined to areas where these natural bog bases are located. Northern Oregon cranberries, for instance, are grown on peat bogs up to 30 feet deep which were producing wild berries when Lewis and Clark first traded with the Indians for them in November of 1805.

Oregon coast cranberry growers have borrowed from the timber industry in developing efficient harvesting machinery. With the water reel, the bogs are flooded and the reels rotated to agitate the surface and are pushed by long booms toward a submerged hopper in the same way logs are manipulated toward mill belts. Conveyors then lift them to the trucks.

Bog workers wear unique stilt shoes made by fastening wooden platforms with short wooden pegs to the soles of their boots, enabling them to walk through the vines without trampling the berries.

In late September Bandon hosts its annual **Cranberry Festival** complete with the usual trappings: a parade, the coronation of a queen, and a barbecue in the park. A Cranberry Fair is held in conjunction with the festival where local ladies bring homemade cranberry goods for sale: jams, breads, cakes, candies and more. Tours of the cranberry bogs are conducted during the harvest season when the "crimson ponds" are at their most colorful. The Bandon Chamber of Commerce coordinates the trips. Tours of the Ocean Spray processing facilities may be arranged also, subject to seasonal conditions, by contacting the company offices in Bandon.

Special Side Trips

Some short side trips can add an extra dimension to a visit in Bandon. From Bandon's Old Town the **Beach Loop Road** — several miles of scenic secondary highway — ambles through rural countryside of small homesteads that seem to have survived from a quieter era. Some parts of it have survived for eons. The beaches are studded with great rock formations, remnants of a historic coastline. **Face Rock**, a giant natural carving shaped by ocean currents, resembles the face of a legendary Indian Princess, turned to stone by an evil spirit.

Fields of sandy land are covered with waving shore grasses which in early spring are frosted with hazy blue, invaded by hordes of wildflowers. There are stopping places along the way from which to view the abandoned lighthouse, a small white toy of a building on the tideflats below the road which would be more at home in Eugene Field's *Land of Counterpane*. Yellow scotch broom, covering the hilly road heights in season, makes a lovely frame for color photographs of the tiny light station at the mouth of the Coquille, a landmark since 1896, and open to the public from the north side of the river.

The road follows a long, lovely beach before rejoining Highway 101. It is a perfect route for bikers and hikers.

A cruise up the Coquille River on the river boat **Bold Duck** is an excursion into yesterday. Twice-daily cruises leave the Bandon docks for two-hour excursions past Indian burial grounds and old shipyards, log ponds and mill sites and ferries and shipyards six miles or so up the Coquille River and back. Weekend dinner cruises depart at 5:30 pm. The ticket office on the waterfront in Old Town Bandon is open 11:00 am to 3:00 pm daily.

Stern-wheelers are nothing new on the Coquille; river boats had served as the major transportation system since the mid-1800's until a graveled road was completed in the 1920's connecting Myrtle Point, a few miles upriver from Coquille, with Bandon on the coast.

A pleasant 17-mile drive from Bandon on Highway 42S follows the river to the historic community of **Coquille** through an area of productive farmlands and dairies and small mills bordering the deep-flowing Coquille River.

A treasure trove of historic buildings are in everyday use in the town: the **Nosler House** and the **Paulson/Mauney House** on Elliot Street, for example, dating back to the 1890's (the latter with a striking conical-roofed tower); the striking **Luckey Bonney House**, an outstanding example of Queen Anne architecture built in 1901. The **Coquille Valley Sentinel**, the weekly newspaper that has been published continually since 1882, is housed in a delightful old building at No. 1 Barton's Alley, once a bank whose vault is now used as a storage area.

The Myrtle Burl on West Central Boulevard (entering Coquille on Highway 42S) was established in the 1930's by Charles Oerding and his wife Lois when the family business, started by his father in 1909, was discontinued. Charles, a master craftsman in myrtlewood manufacture, began working with the unusual wood as a child of 10 in his father's myrtlewood factory. The lovely pieces for sale here reflect the special care with which they are produced. There is a variety of gift items here, but it is the myrtlewood that holds the spotlight.

Coquille is also the home of **The Sawdusters**, who have presented a summer season of old time vaudeville with the now-famous production of **The Drunkard** for the past 20 years.

West Coast Game Farm is a treat for old and young alike. There are few fences. The deer roam the park at will, as do sheep and goats; and there are exotic animals from around the world. This walk-through zoo encourages children to pet the livestock. And there are no DO NOT FEED THE ANIMAL signs in evidence; quite the contrary. Over 400 birds and animals are here to be observed close up in a natural setting. Adventurous kids of all ages can take a ride on a water buffalo; those less daring can opt for pony rides. The game park, located seven miles south of Bandon, is an experience most visitors to the area won't want to miss.

Annual Events

Old Fashioned Fourth of July Celebration
Cranberry Festival — September

Notes:

PORT ORFORD

Port Orford, the most westerly incorporated city in the continental United States, is a self-styled "working fishing village" of 1,100 people halfway between Bandon and Gold Beach. It is situated on the only natural deepwater harbor between San Francisco and Seattle.

The atmosphere is pleasantly relaxed here — a curious legacy for a community established after a bloody confrontation between a group of settlers and hostile Indians, who placed a one-hundred-year hex on the city after they were defeated by the intruders.

The colonists were men recruited in Portland, Oregon, in the spring of 1851 by merchant Captain William Tichenor, who planned to set up a trade station to supply the gold miners already operating in the region. Armed with handguns and a tiny cannon, the men were unloaded on a huge stone mound resembling a lumpy loaf of bread in the harbor. Cut from the mainland by high tides, the rock offered the most defensible site along the beach where the unfriendly Indians were gathering to watch their landing.

Captain Tichenor planned to return within two weeks with supplies and reinforcements. The ship was barely out of the harbor before the Indians began harassment. The attack which followed was repulsed by the colonists but left some settlers wounded and several Indians dead.

The isolated white men managed to hold the Indians at bay for two weeks with promises to be gone at the end of that time. On the fifteenth day, with no relief ship in evidence, between three and four hundred Indians gathered on the beach and charged the rock a second time. Again the settlers held their own but, with ammunition running low, decided to make a run for it. They pretended to begin construction of a fort on the rock to draw attention of the Indians from their escape plans. When the Indians who were keeping watch over the intruders' activities left the rock unguarded to report the new developments to the warring chiefs, the embattled men escaped from the rock and went overland to the settlement on the Umpqua River to the north.

Three weeks overdue, Captain Tichenor finally landed sixty-seven armed men at the site who built a blockhouse and established the present city.

Three weeks overdue, Captain Tichenor finally landed sixty-seven armed men at the site who built a blockhouse and established the present city, overlooking Battle Rock.

Myrtlewood shops are as plentiful as sand dollars along the Oregon coast, where the world's major supply of the rare hardwood grows. The wood, marked with unusual grain patterns, aglow with colors ranging from soft yellows through sand beiges and warm browns, seems to come alive in the hands of master craftsmen. Today's woodcrafters are transforming the manufacture of myrtlewood pieces from folk art to fine art. The varnish-glazed bowls and lamp bases that once comprised the selections available are being preempted by tableware and designer accessories and furnishings of classic elegance with soft satiny finishes.

The Wooden Nickel on Highway 101 at the north end of Port Orford offers superior examples of the myrtlewood pieces along with other fine crafts items displayed in innovative cases and racks as interesting as the contents: hanging racks for stenciled T-shirts (baby through X-large) fashioned from large wooden wheels, for instance.

The myrtlewood pieces come in varied styles and patterns and sizes: bowls and plates and trays and compotes — some basic, some handled or pedestled or lidded; condiment sets and cheese trays and candle holders and vases; turned clocks and such. Designer plates centered with laser carvings delicate as fine lace, depicting coastal trees and shore scenes, are treasures. An expandable myrtlewood holder (books or napkins or papers) of unique design is a different gift, practical as well as decorative. Small weed vases make charming souvenirs.

In short, this is probably the most varied collection of myrtlewood pieces to be found under one roof on the Oregon coast.

On the corner where the highway turns to dip downhill is located the workshop and salesroom of **Knutson's Handcrafted Clocks**. Lyle and Margaret Knutson create the elegant timepieces from exotic woods — black walnut, acacia, maple and myrtlewood, to name a few — with loving care. The wood is selected and the design is created to highlight the grain in each piece chosen. Mantle clocks, grandfather, grandmother (a chiming wall clock) even a mother-in-law clock, are basic styles; but custom orders are encouraged by these talented people who enjoy creating one-of-a-kind masterpieces to individual tastes.

Walking into the showroom filled with these magnificent creations is a little like walking into a childhood memory of Santa's workshop. One has the impression, talking with the Knutsons against the background of muted chimes and tickings, that each is an individual personality to them; that placing a beautiful clock in the hands of an admiring purchaser is, for them, akin to the feeling parents know in seeing a daughter married to the "right" husband.

The Oregon myrtlewood grandfather clock is their most popular item. Prices start, believe it or not, at a moderate $17.50. But there is no lack of buyers for the works of art created from luxury woods which, of necessity, places some of them in the four-figure price range.

On the beach side of the highway, just past the sharp turn, is **Walter's Landing Leather**. The specialty here is custom leather goods. Since 1974, when the Walters opened their business, it has grown "year by year, month by month." Among leather goods manufactured here from scratch are sheepskin slippers, designed by Walters, made from tanned skins with the wool left on to form a cuddly, inch-thick lining. Hats made of sheepskin are designed in the same manner with the wool inside for warmth and comfort. All goods made here are carefully crafted for style and durability.

A pleasant gift shop, **From Oregon With Love** carries a variety of distinctive gifts — fine glass, including figurines; books, cards, and prints and crafts — representative of the talents of Oregon artists and artisans. The owners "try to keep prices down to where residents can afford to shop here," good news for visitors to the area.

Port Orford is not lacking in restaurants. At the top of the list or very near is **The Truculant Oyster**, serving excellent food local residents are willing to wait in line for. This dinner house is attractive, but there is no view. The quality of the menu makes up for it.

The Galley Cafe across the street has a specialty highly advertised and all too seldom delivered: *good homemade food*! It's a plain, homey little place but you can't beat their pies! It's a friendly place, too. And the prices are right.

Madelaine's Bed and Breakfast on the corner where the highway turns is easily spotted in a large house of an earlier era. It is beautifully furnished with "livable" antiques, with charming decorating accents: hall walls hung with hand-pieced quilts; the round dining table centered with a hand-crocheted cloth. Hand braided rugs cover the floor; an old brass bedstead gleams in one bedroom; another sports a decorative white iron headboard. Breakfast is served by the lady of the house; or can be prepared by visitors in the old-fashioned kitchen furnished with an old-fashioned cook stove. Rates here are surprisingly moderate.

Home by the Sea overlooking the harbor on Jackson Street, offers accommodations (two rooms) in a new contemporary home with a striking fireplace wall and a superb ocean view that can be enjoyed while sitting by the hearth. Kitchen and laundry facilities are included. Both rooms have private baths and a continental breakfast is served as part of the package. Nonsmokers will appreciate their request that guests step outside to light up.

The Neptune Motel on the heights overlooking the Port Orford dock area offers a magnificent ocean vista from the private glass sun porches which front the guest suites.

Some special "homes away from home" are available to vacationers in the Port Orford area. **The Neptune Motel** stretches along the top of a high crest overlooking the dock area, presenting a spectacular view of harbor, mountains, and beaches. Private suites (one or three bedroom) are fronted with glassed-in sun porches; larger suites have circular wrought iron staircases leading to upstairs bedrooms. Electric fireplaces add to a sense of warmth and comfort while watching ocean storms. And when seas run high, visitors may watch Port Orford's "fleet on wheels" being hoisted out of the water by giant cranes.

Pathways and wooden stairs lead directly to the docks from the motel grounds, for hikers or fishing enthusiasts. Restaurants, galleries, and shops are within walking distance. For fine accommodations with what may well be the most spectacular view of the southern Oregon coastline, the Neptune is the choice.

Fiddleback Manor on the cliffs directly across the harbor, can properly be referred to as "the height of luxury." The private resort is truly extraordinary. Begin with a hilltop ranch house built from a Frank Lloyd Wright design, with 80 feet of window wall framing an expanse of ocean vista of breathtaking beauty. Combine it with decor and furnishings of distinctive style; surround it with ten acres of natural landscaping that ensures privacy without isolation (Port Orford shops and restaurants are just minutes away at the foot of the hill). Embellish it with luxurious extras — music room with satellite TV, VCR; electric kitchen with microwave and table service for twelve, with a formal dining room of comparable capacity; plus complimentary champagne, evening snacks and first-morning breakfast materials waiting on arrival,. Together they add up to Fiddleback — in a class by itself.

A visit to the **Prehistoric Gardens**, located midway between Port Orford and Gold Beach, offers a unique experience. The gardens, showing lifelike scale models of prehistoric animals in a natural rain forest setting, is one of the most unusual presentations of its kind in the world.

Developed by E.V. and Kari Nelson to scientific standards based on years of research, the replicas are posed among moss-draped trees hundreds of years old in thickets of ferns suggestive of jungle forests, and along the banks of creeks and pools thick with outsized vegetation. One skunk cabbage found in the park had leaves measuring up to seven feet in length.

Many visitors following the quiet paths among the natural dioramas bathed in a continually changing light show of sun and shadow are overwhelmed by a feeling of being lost in a segment of forgotten time. The exhibit is far more than a series of statues standing among the trees. The Nelsons have captured a sense of reality, in the way the models in an excellent wax museum seem "real." The creatures have been captured in "living" poses. One especially effective scene shows a pair examining a nest on the ground — one standing upright carefully cradling an egg, the other stooping to examine a broken shell. One somehow receives the impression of young parents returning to find their home has been violated.

After measuring skeletons in museums and studying the works of artist Charles R. Knight, famed for his paintings of prehistoric animals, Nelson constructed the models by shaping frames of steel and metal lath which were plastered with concrete and painted to complete the natural appearance. Technical advice was obtained from the Department of Anthropology at the University of Oregon. Over the years Nelson has collected an extensive paleontology library.

Unobtrusive plaques inserted in man-made stones give statistics and information relative to the exhibits. "The first tree-like plants two or three feet high evolved near the ocean's edge over 400 million years ago . . ." or "There are more than 10,000 species of ferns . . ." The creatures themselves are named and profiled briefly at each site.

Life-scale models of long-vanished creatures are posed among moss-draped trees hundreds of years old in the Prehistoric Gardens. The models are constructed of steel and concrete plaster after painstaking research through museums and other scientific sources. Plaques set into man-made rocks give basic information about the animals and the ancient environment in which they developed. This educational exhibit is one of the most fascinating along the Oregon coast and is located half-way between Port Orford and Gold Beach.

The project was started in 1953 and is still evolving. A gift shop carries souvenir items which depict or relate to prehistoric animals. The Nelsons scout gift fairs on buying trips searching for worthwhile items. Dinosaurs, popular as mementos, are harder and harder to come by. Some replicas are still obtainable from Korea; some are hand-carved in Mexico from onyx; others are imported from Spain. But they are becoming scarce, and prices, as with almost everything else, have climbed steadily in the past few years. In desperation Nelson designed a baby dinosaur which is being used on gift items and souvenirs for sale. The shop was enlarged in 1978.

E.V. Nelson, a self-described "forger and steeler" (he manufactured logging equipment for twenty years) has turned a lifelong interest in prehistoric creatures into an educational tourist attraction — one well worth exploring. A moderate charge keeps the Prehistoric Gardens within family vacation budgets.

Arizona Beach is one of the few resorts on the Oregon coast offering RV camping at the ocean's edge. The 200 sites along the beach in the campground allow RVers to step out of doors directly onto the sand. Spread at the base of coastal mountains, the park also has more sheltered spaces among the trees and meadows back from the shore.

But the sound of the surf will lull travelers to sleep from anywhere in the spacious resort, and the sea smell follows campers who explore the remnants of the old Stage Road near the location of the famous Arizona Beach Inn, an important stop on the stage route that linked California and Oregon coastal towns. The Old Inn building burned in 1942, but the site is marked by a lovely shade tree that bears a plaque noting its historic background.

Arizona Beach Resort offers comprehensive facilities; in addition to RV spaces there are modern motel units, some with kitchens, plus an activity hall which is reserved often for family reunions. Tent spaces are also available.

All camp sites have electric hookups. Beach spaces, for obvious reasons, have no sewer hookups, but a dumping station on the grounds accommodates self-contained RVs. Gas and propane are for sale to campers.

This is a pleasant locale for a vacation stop, whether for a day or a week or an entire summer. The private beach affords swimming, surf fishing, beachcombing for driftwood and agate. A private road connects the main park with the beach by means of a highway underpass, a safety feature appreciated by parents. Nearby scenic mountain trails offer plenty of opportunity for hiking. And the Prehistoric Gardens are a short walk from the resort store.

Located midway between Port Orford and Gold Beach, Arizona Beach is one of the most popular campgrounds on the southern coast. During the four summer months visitors number well into the thousands. However, the resort is open the year around, and many groups take advantage of the less-crowded seasons for get-togethers. It is recommended that reservations for the summer season or for special holidays be made three months in advance. But whenever guests arrive, they will enjoy the very special hospitality at Arizona Beach.

Cape Blanco State Park north of Port Orford is the site of Oregon's highest lighthouse (250 feet above sea level) as well as the farthest west. The key-shaped headland is surrounded by black-sand beaches, unusual in the state, which are choice hunting grounds for rockhounds and beachcombers.

Humbug Mountain State Park, 6 miles south of Port Orford, has picnic sites (30+) and camping areas (75 tent, 30 trailer) in a park-like setting. Beach access is via a highway underpass from the park. A 3-mile trail leads to the top of Humbug Mountain, which rises 1,750 feet above sea level.

Annual Events

Jubilee Celebration — July Fourth

Notes:

Low tide is the best time to seek out the elusive razor clams, most popular of the varieties found on the Oregon coast. Clammers must move fast to catch the razors which can disappear into the beach sand at the rate of 30 seconds/foot.

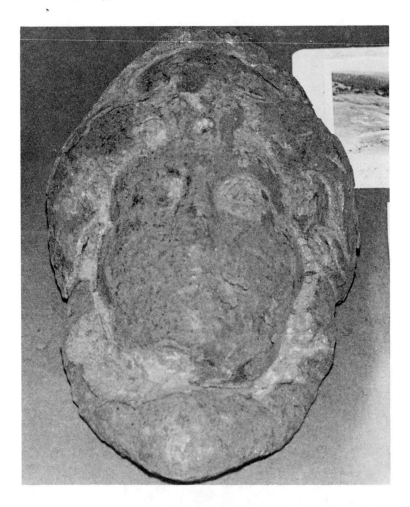

The most interesting exhibit in the Chetco Valley Museum in Brookings is an ancient iron mask, a casting of a woman's face. Discovered on Lone Ranch Beach in 1957, journalists speculate on the possibility that it may be a likeness of Britain's Queen Elizabeth, left near the site by Sir Francis Drake during his run along the northern coast nearly 400 years earlier.

Sea Explorers of the Oregon Coast

The Pacific Northwest Coast was one of the world's last major coastlines to be explored (barring the Arctic areas), and Oregon's was the end of the line. True, as early as the mid-16th century Spanish navigators had cautiously crept north from their bases in Latin America, but barely past the California border. Juan Cabrillo in 1542 reached a point to the north of San Francisco bay; and there is some indication that his pilot Ferrelo may have taken his small vessel a few degrees farther north—enough to have crossed the Oregon boundary latitude at 42 degrees—after Cabrillo's death put him in command. But if either man made a landing, it has not been noted in any known records.

Thirty-six years later Sir Francis Drake, the renowned buccaneer in the service of Queen Elizabeth at the advent of Great Britain's challenge to Spain for supremacy of the world's oceans, made a recorded landing on the California coast north of San Francisco. It's possible that he also made a brief landfall on the Oregon coast on the same voyage.

Stuffed to the gunwales with treasure from surprise raids on the Spaniard's Pacific ports, Drake's *Golden Hind*—100 tons capacity with a crew of 60—wallowed north along the California coastline to avoid retaliation from Spanish officials undoubtedly on the alert for the pirate ship's return by the southern route.

It's improbable that exploration was uppermost in Drake's mind at the time; not much was known of what lay to the north. But given his alternatives, he may have been taking a chance on finding the fabled Northwest Passage whose existence had been rumored since Magellan completed his circling of the globe in 1522. In any case, Drake is credited with naming the upper Pacific coastal area "New Albion," a designation which held for 200 years or more.

Records of Drake's voyage give conflicting coordinates for the northern point reached during his journey. By his own account dated June 3, 1578, the ship sailed into cold and fog which held for two weeks before he backtracked south to a small bay just north of San Francisco, making it impossible to chart course by either sun or stars. Estimates place his one northern landing between 43 and 48 degrees latitude, but either would be along the Oregon coast, and possibly the "bad bay" in which he was forced to seek shelter from the winds is located there.

His descriptions of extreme cold, barren shores, and snow-covered mountains read more like the Arctic than Oregon's "banana belt" south coast, but historians still speculate that the great explorer, knighted by Queen Elizabeth on his return from the three-year journey of conquest, may have landed somewhere in the vicinity of Cape Arago. And it was on the basis of his account of the trip up the Pacific coast that the English based future claims to ownership of the Oregon Country.

In 1602 Sebastian Viscaino, under orders from King Philip II of Spain, headed an expedition from Mexico to establish a colony in lower California. After discovery of the Bay of Monterey, a storm separated one of the three ships in the expedition. Viscaino went north to 42 degrees latitude and reported seeing "white bluffs" of a promontory which are generally considered to have been the present Cape Blanco.

Commander d'Aguilar of the separated frigate, believing Viscaino was still proceeding north when he had indeed turned south again, continued in that direction and logged the first written description of the Oregon coast at somewhere north of 43 degrees. It was d'Aguilar who gave the name of Blanco to the headland he described, but he also reported near it a river large enough to prevent the ship entering it for fresh water. There is no river near Cape Blanco (or Cape Orford as it was later named by Lt. Vancouver in 1792). And d'Aguilar thought the river which they could not enter might be the famous Strait of Anian, or the Northwest Passage, between the Atlantic and Pacific oceans. It is believed by some historians that the river he saw may have been the Umpqua to the north.

It was almost 175 years before another landing was made (perhaps) on the Oregon coast. In March, 1775, an expedition of two Spanish ships commanded by Bruno Heceta and Juan Francisco de Bodega y Quadra, on a voyage of exploration out of Mexico, landed somewhere north of Cape Mendocino, again possibly in Oregon. Storms swept them out to sea on leaving their sheltered bay, taking them north to the coast of Washington before another landing could be made.

On the return voyage down the coast on August 17, 1775, Heceta anchored off the mouth of the Columbia, at first believing it to be the legendary Strait of Juan de Fuca, not yet located although it had long been marked on existing maps. He logged his anchorage at 45 degrees and decided this could not be the strait supposedly found by a Greek ship's pilot Apostolos Valerianos (who used the name Juan de Fuca) while on a voyage of exploration in 1592, which was recorded as being between 47-48 degrees latitude. Although the titanic currents and blasting winds made it impossible for Heceta to enter the estuary, his description of the beaches, land conformations, and especially of Neahkahnie Mountain leave no doubt of his location.

Three years later on March 7, 1778, Captain James Cook, the English navigator, attempted a landing at Yaquina Bay. But storms kept him tacking along the coast looking for a harbor, and resulted in his naming Cape Foulweather below Depoe Bay for his frustrating experience, and Cape Perpetua for the Saint who had been martyred on that date 1600 years earlier.

Ultimately, he reached Nootka Bay on the west shore of Vancouver Island, having missed the mouth of the Columbia altogether. But before leaving the north seas, he sailed into the

Arctic Ocean until solid ice stopped his ship and dispelled once and for all the existence of the Northwest Passage connecting the world's two major oceans.

It was another 14 years before the American Captain Robert Gray finally found courage to take a ship over the bar through terrifying currents and crashing waves into the mighty river which, if not the Northwest Passage, served as one of the principal waterways for east-west traffic over the American continent before railroads tied the two coasts together with steel tracks.

And were it not for the capricious weather for which the Columbia River bar is famous (or infamous), it might today be known as Rio Heceta, after the Spanish name given the estuary for many years on the maps of Spain—Ensenada Heceta.

A driftwood shelter makes a snug harbor from the wind. Shelters are seen on most Oregon beaches which boast a collection of driftwood.

The southern Oregon coast has a solitary beauty far removed from the activity of the upper coast areas, where wild breakers froth and pound at the ragged headlands. The stark crags to the south seem almost untouched by these tremendous natural forces; as if, having been shaped through past ages to the bare bones structures they now assume, they stand impervious to further assaults from seas that thunder around them with the force of liquid mountains.

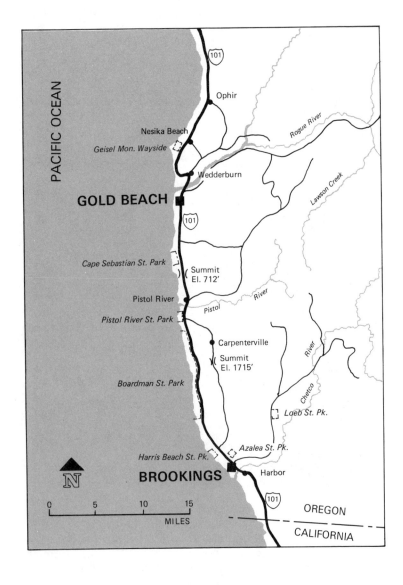

Gold Beach
Brookings

GOLD BEACH

Gold Beach/Wedderburn bracket the mouth of the world-famous Rogue River, one of the nation's ten "wild" waterways — Wedderburn on the north, Gold Beach on the south. **Gold Beach** is named for the gold found there by the miners who first settled the area. The community of Wedderburn was established by Robert D. Hume, who owned much of the land along the lower Rogue River at one time. Known as "the salmon king of the Rogue," Hume dominated the commercial salmon fishing in the area. When his cannery at Gold Beach was destroyed by fire, he floated the buildings which were saved across the river and set them up on the north bank of the river's mouth and continued his operations from the site of what is now the community of **Wedderburn**.

The Wild River

In early morning **The Rogue**, the focal point for the Gold Beach area, is hushed, mist-shrouded, as it nears its rendezvous with the Pacific. An hour later passengers will board the jet boats that will take them upriver thirty miles through an incomparable scenic wilderness; or carry them on another twenty miles into threshing white water and churning rapids channeled through narrow, rock-walled canyons. But for now the empty river craft move gently with the water's lapping. A seagull settles atop a piling to which one boat is tied and rests there; across the placid river mouth, cattle browse in an island meadow.

Soon enough the activity begins which will launch the morning trip. First down the skeletal ramp to the low floating docks is the dairyman carting boxes of milk — first of a series of delivery men who will load supplies for the isolated river lodges upstream.

Shortly after his appearance the passengers begin to desert the free coffee in the small booking office for the mini-decks that overlook the boats. They all wear jackets (the morning is cool) and hats (protection against a later sunburn). Many carry cameras and sunglasses.

A few minutes before the 8:30 departure time, the pilots, professional guides and boatmen, come down the ramp and wait to assist the passengers who follow into the open boat. When all are seated comfortably, the engines thrust to life, the boat makes a sweeping curve into the current, and the trip has begun.

The ride to **Agness**, terminal of the half-day trips is a leisurely scenic journey through country which gradually makes the transformation from coastal environment to river wilderness. Traveling by boat affords a different perspective than is gained from the hill road which curves and winds along the rim of the cliffs bordering the river. Along the lower Rogue the green of fir and cedar, oak and madrona are softened by the paler greens of wild shrubs. In spring fuchsia and azaleas gleam in Easter-egg pinks and oranges among the green; wild iris and ceanothus make "dilly-dilly" patches of lavender-blue, highlighted by the sun-yellow of buttercup and mustard. In September the fiery reds of Indian paintbrush and patimous burn boldly on the hillsides.

A camera is a must on the river trip up the Rogue. Where else could a photographer have a ringside seat to "shoot" a half dozen fresh-water otter sharing a dinner of just-caught

The last passengers are helped aboard the boat, eager to begin the six-hour trip up the scenic Rogue River, which will include a leisurely lunch at world-famous Lucas Lodge, a landmark on the Rogue for over 75 years.

salmon on a river rock? Boat pilots pull inshore and stop frequently for such sideshows, giving passengers close-ups of deer, bear, coyotes, and sometimes wild pig, plus beaver, raccoon, and once in a while, elk. The river is a paradise for bird lovers also, harboring osprey, golden eagles, blue heron, and snowy egrets among the countless varieties of bird life along its shores.

Historical landmarks too are seen along the way: sites of Indian confrontations during the years of unrest among the Rogues; crumbling artifacts abandoned by miners who were the Rogue's first settlers. The pilots, well versed in local lore, are glad to answer questions.

High spot of the trip may well be lunch at historic **Lucas Ranch** at Agness, the old farmhouse turned lodge where, for over seventy-five years, the Lucas family has been serving home-cooked meals from their own garden products to river travelers. Founded by Larry Lucas, long-time unofficial "Mayor of the Rogue," it is now operated by his son Willard, who has tried hard to keep it unchanged. The food is served family style in the long glassed-in dining room where tables and benches are covered in red bandana-patterned oil cloth. Old kerosene lanterns and lamps hang from the ceiling beams, until recent years the only lighting for evening dining.

It is not unusual for the lodge to feed up to 150 guests at a sitting. And it's safe to say the fame of Lucas' homegrown, home-cooked meals have spread around the globe by word of mouth through famed personages who, like President Herbert Hoover, have fished and boated the Rogue. Many, having experienced the beauty of the region, have become residents; among them western writer Zane Gray and, more recently, the lovely film star Ginger Rogers.

There is time at the noon stop for passengers to relax in the outdoor courtyard ringed by great shade trees and "furnished" with tables made of thick slabs of native logs. To one side a grapevine a hundred years old roofs a room-sized trellis.

They'll have time, too, to pick up incidentals or mementos at the small store in the front of the lodge. Some may even want to explore the Agness "airport" — a small landing strip centering a pasture beyond the Lucas vegetable garden, which may require pilots to chase grazing cattle off the runway before takeoff.

If Lucas Ranch is the granddaddy of Rogue resorts, **Singing Springs**, alternate meal stop at Agness for the jet trips, is a most attractive young adult in its twenties. Singing Springs Ranch offers modern guest cottages with private baths and view windows — even porches — mid-April to mid-November.

Owners Rudy and Delores Valenta feature home-cooked meals served outdoors "with a smile" to boat passengers, who may also enjoy wine and beer in the charming patio shaded by old myrtlewood and fir trees. Passengers will have time here to look around the naturally landscaped ranch gardens, or to browse the distinctive gift shop.

Both morning and afternoon trips, six hours long, are made to Agness, terminal point of the original mail boat run which began in 1895 to provide postal service to settlers who were inaccessible by road. An all-day trip carries passengers twenty miles farther upriver into rocky channels boiling with white water, as far as Paradise Canyon where rock cliffs loom 1,500 feet above the river's surface. Boats making the trip beyond Agness, where the "truly wild river" begins, are small, designed to challenge the unruly Rogue on its own terms, piloted by licensed guides who know the upper river well.

For all the rugged, untamed beauty of the Rogue, the river trips are safe and comfortable. All jet craft making the runs are manufactured at Gold Beach to rigid Coast Guard standards. They vary in size from ten to thirty-five passenger capacity. Pilots on all river boats must pass Coast Guard examinations before being certified.

Companies operating the Rogue River jet boat trips are both located at the mouth of the river; **Jerry's Rogue River Jet Boats** on the south side of the bridge in Gold Beach; **Courts White Water Trips**; **Rogue River Mail Boat Trips** (pioneer mail service begun in 1895, with passenger service since the 1930's) both on the north side of the river at Wedderburn.

Reservations are not required, but are advisable, for boat trips and for lunch or dinner at the upriver resorts, especially during the summer season.

Tu Tu Tun Vacation Lodge seven miles upriver on the north bank of the Rogue is one of the finest on the coast. Fishing for the world-famous Chinook salmon and steelhead is one of the main attractions offered by this superior resort, but it is only one of the many features that make it unique.

The rustic modern buildings overlooking the river house a central lobby which boasts a wall-sized rock fireplace, a cozy lodge, and a dining room which features round tables (comfortable for six) with lazy susan turntables for convenient home-style serving. The menu offers fresh meats, seafood, and vegetables and fruits, and there are always snacks at hand between times. Breakfast is served early for those who are eager to get out on the river, and packed lunches will be prepared on order. To top it off, an angler's catch can be the entree for the evening meal if desired.

Rooms are beautifully appointed to reflect the exclusive but casual atmosphere, and each has a private balcony with a river view, plus special racks for fishing equipment and outdoor gear. Drying rooms are there for taking care of wet clothing.

Guests not interested in fishing will find plenty of recreational activity to help them enjoy a perfect stay. A pitch and putt course, horseshoes, and a heated swimming pool are part of the lodge facilities along with a recreation room with an antique pool table and a player piano. Outdoor activities also include horseback riding, a golf course nearby, hiking, excursion boat trips upriver on the jet boats which stop daily at the private dock to pick up guests for the scenic boat trips. Sightseeing flights are available from Pacific Air Services operating out of Gold Beach Airport where both charter and private flights can use the landing strip. Transportation to and from the airport is furnished by the lodge.

Fishermen must bring their own gear, but licenses are obtainable at Tu Tu Tun. For those bringing their own boats, arrangements can be made through the lodge for fishing guides as well as for anglers who wish to hire them. Lodge personnel will also care for the catch and hold it until departure, either fresh or frozen for shipping.

The service at Tu Tu Tun is on the American plan, and rates include three meals a day in addition to lodging. For a vacation which combines exclusive comfort with accessibility to coastal activities, Tu Tu Tun is almost unbeatable.

Some Shops to Explore

The Gull Gallery on Highway 101 north of Gold Beach expresses the discriminating tastes of its owners, not only in the quality gifts they carry but in the decor of the shop itself. From the outside The Gull Gallery resembles many others along the coast. But the interior is another story.

A display wall of random length driftwood shakes provides the perfect background for sand-polished driftwood carvings of coast birds and marine life. Thick ceiling beams of driftwood from an old cannery offer a perfect drop for hangings.

A tone of quality is emphasized throughout the gallery. The scrimshaw chests are exquisite; shells seem special somehow; paintings and drawings hold the interest of the browser from wall to wall.

The Pelican's Pouch contains just about everything the gift buyer could want in the arts/crafts line: jewelry, myrtlewood, pottery, stained glass, paintings, carvings — they're all to be found at one convenient location. The gallery is easy to spot as the traveler enters Gold Beach.

Don't miss **The Glass Apple**, a nearby shop that specializes in fragile things: stained glass of all kinds, lamps, studio windows, plus tools and classes for do-it-yourselfers.

Outstanding is the **Sugar Shoppe**, the chocoholics' dream of a candy store. Along with the large selection of candies one expects to find in such places, this one offers some delightful novelty items. For instance: solid chocolate greeting cards, about four by six inches BIG, with appropriate messages — Happy Birthday or Be My Valentine — surrounded by molded flowers and scrolls. They are thin enough to look like the real things (maybe a quarter of an inch) and thick enough to satisfy the appetite of a true chocolate addict.

They make their own soft-center chocolates, thirty-two flavors, with whipped cream filling, in light and dark coatings. They have also blended an inviting natural fruit bar which is one of the best sugarless confections you'll find anywhere. Dates, figs, seeds, nuts, and honey go into this tasty candy.

You can pick up fine coffees and teas here. And jars of penny candy are placed on low shelves for young customers who like to ponder the choices before blowing their allowances on goodies.

They will ship candies anywhere if postage is included with orders, except during hot weather.

Pleasant Places to Eat

Grant's is a breakfast and lunch place (6:00 am-4:00 pm) offering thirty-five omelets ranging in price from $2.65 - $5.10 (the latter a fisherman's omelet filled with crab, shrimp, or salmon). Several kinds of pancakes and waffles are listed. All regular breakfasts are served with grits if desired. An assortment of sandwiches listed includes avocado with bacon and a Spanish burger, both good. Grant's is located a short distance off the highway on the south side of the river, next door to Indian Creek Campground (take the first turn left as you come off the bridge from the north).

The Captain's Table at the south end of Gold Beach on Highway 101 is recommended. An interesting decor makes for a pleasant atmosphere; the food is excellent. Try this one.

The Golden Egg serves breakfast all day. From 6:00 am to 9:00 pm seven days a week they prepare an assortment of exotic omelets on order. The Golden Egg is easy to find on South Ellensburg Street (Highway 101).

Riley's On The Rogue, noted for the fine seafood and steaks served in the restaurant, also offers motel accommodations and facilities for trailers, plus a dock and tackle shop. The dining room is open 5:00 to 10:00 pm. Riley's is located a mile off Highway 101 on the South Bank Road.

Jot's Resort on the north bank of the river offers rooms, restaurant, and lounge, plus boat rentals and a sports shop. Court's White Water Trips jet boats depart from their docks for the daily run up the Rogue.

Some Special Parking Places

Operators of **Indian Creek Recreation Park** may not be able to offer everything to make campers happy, but they sure give it a good try. From the moment an RVer turns into the attractive grounds overlooking the mouth of the Rogue River, he'll feel welcome.

Many of the one hundred hookups for RVers are clustered around central shelters which offer the perfect set-up for family reunions or ground camping. And there is a special section for tenters among the natural wooded areas at the back of the park.

Vacationers could spend weeks at Indian Creek without leaving the grounds if they were a mind to. The laundry, store (groceries and gifts), and Pancake House are just a stroll away from the hookup sites. In the lodge building is an upstairs recreation room with pool tables, a piano, television, and games of all kinds. There are outside activity areas for both children and adults, too. Both the recreation room and the outdoor barbeque can be reserved for private parties.

But it is the little extras that make this park special. The park office personnel will give guests information on all restaurants in the vicinity, including copies of their menus; will help guests find a baby sitter, or point them in the direction of a beauty shop. They have an activity list of things to do in the Gold Beach area and will even make reservations for guests if they are required. Best of all, prices are most reasonable in spite of the special attention they give their patrons.

It's a good place to settle in for a night or a week, or even longer. Indian Creek Park is easy to find a half mile from the highway on the south bank of the Rogue.

Sandy Camp on Ocean Side Drive in Gold Beach offers attractive accommodations for RVers from May through October. Available are thirty-five modern pull-through hookups and fifty self-contained spaces with hot showers, restrooms, and garbage service. There is no extra charge for cars or pets. Prices are computed on a basic charge per vehicle and persons, but they are leveled off at a maximum charge per party, which is most reasonable. Bait and tackle and ice are also available here at this camp near the beaches. Office hours are 8:00 am to 9:00 pm for visitors' convenience.

The Mary D. Hume, after almost a hundred years of adventuresome activity along the Northwest coast of the United States and Alaska, returned to her birthplace for permanent retirement. Visitors can inspect the Mary D. on special occasions; she is always on view for photographs on the south side of the Rogue River near the bridge.

The Pioneer

If the **Mary D. Hume** had been a human instead of a schooner, she would have become a female soldier of fortune. A native Oregonian, she derived from good pioneer stock. Her birthplace was a small cove near Mill Rock at the south end of the bridge over the Rogue at Gold Beach. Her ancestors had no peers. Her keel, 10 feet by 36 feet by 140 feet, was hand-squared from a majestic Douglas fir and floated down the Rouge from Lobster Creek to the building site. But like many a frontier lady she began life using some "pre-tested" accoutrements: her engine was a hand-me-down from an older sister-ship which came to a bad end at an early age, wrecked after a single trip to San Francisco.

The Mary D. made her own way to San Francisco in February of 1881, but during her early years made most of her calls in smaller "dog hole" ports delivering materials loaded out of the glamorous California harbor. And when, after eight years of freight runs along the northern coast, the Pacific Steam Whaling Company bought her for duty in the far North, the Mary D. Hume, smallest ship in the company fleet, moved into her new role with zest.

Refitted and refurbished to handle a cargo of whalebone, she headed for the Arctic, there to spend twenty-nine months — one of the first whalers to be ice-locked into a winter-long station. And also like many a lady who sought her fortunes in the frozen North, she came home with a treasure valued at $400,000, the most lucrative cargo in the history of American whaling.

Details of her career following her whaling days are sketchy, but what facts do emerge indicate the feisty adventuress was not subdued after retiring as a star of the whaling fleet to resume a lesser role as a commercial tug between Puget Sound and Alaska. In 1904 she was sunk by ice in the Nushgak River which empties into Alaska's Bristol Bay, but was rescued and taken to Seattle for repairs; later turning up as a halibut fishing boat for a brief unprofitable venture before returning to tugging and log-raft towing.

But, as it will, time overtook the gallant lady as she went into her nineties, and the Mary D., which once had been known for her triumphant *firsts* began to be noticed for her *lasts*.

She was among the few tugs who still sounded bells on Puget Sound when the ships' bells were silenced by changes in maritime procedures in 1970. At the time of her retirement by the American Tugboat Company in 1977, the Mary D. was the oldest commercial tug still working on the West Coast, and the last survivor of the American fleet of Arctic steam whalers.

Still, hers was not to be the fate of many a footloose lady forced to live out her declining years as a stranger in a strange land. Crowley Maritime Corporation, owner of the Mary D. Hume, made sure the grand old lady of the Northwest coastal waters would spend her remaining days among loved ones in the country of her origin by presenting her to the Curry County Historical Society and the Port of Gold Beach.

On August 31, 1979, at high tide near high noon, the Mary D. Hume, escorted by two forty-four-foot Coast Guard boats and a minor parade of small craft, returned to the Rogue River as hundreds of spectators lined the jetties to applaud her final entry into her home port.

The Mary D. Hume rests there now, and visitors can see her rocking gently in her berth within sight of her birthplace — the land originally owned by Robert D. Hume, Rogue River's salmon king, who christened her over a hundred years ago as the namesake of his wife, Mary Duncan Hume.

BROOKINGS

Brookings, just 7 miles north of the California border, is the southern gateway city for the Oregon coast. **Brookings Harbor**, one of the safest on the coast, is a fascinating place to be in late afternoon when the fishing boats return from their day's work to the modern port facilities — berths for sports craft in addition to the 150 commercial fishing vessels based here.

Nearby **Sporthaven Park** is one of the few sites along the coast where RVers can step out of their mobile "homes away from home" and be within spitting distance of the ocean. Located on a sandy spit which banks the Brookings boat basin from the Pacific, Sporthaven is a perfect spot for those who come to fish, and a fun stopover for travelers who want an interesting spot in which to stop for the night.

The jetty provides a natural grandstand for watching the boats come trundling in to shore as the day begins to fade, and also offers ideal perches for anglers. Photographers find the basin a delight, with small craft in Easter-egg colors lined up along the docks near tall-masted sailing vessels. Fish cleaning stations, ice, gas and picnicking facilities are also available.

At the end of the spit sits the **Chetco River Coast Guard Station**. Near the buildings is a small memorial to the 10 Coast Guard crewmen who were lost in a storm August 16, 1972, honoring specifically the two who were never found.

Also located on Lower Harbor Road is the **Driftwood Travel Trailer Retreat**. The name is well chosen. The RVers stopping here are sheltered by shade trees while still having easy access to the beach. The all-electric hookup and drive-through spaces are quiet and secluded; a laundry and a recreation room are conveniently located.

The park owners offer an added activity to fishing and beachcombing for those who wish to spend longer periods of time in their pleasant surroundings: free classes in driftwood art.

On Highway 101 the **Chetco Travel Trailer Resort**, a mile south of the Chetco Bridge, offers over 100 drive-through spaces and 96 hookups, plus adult recreational facilities and laundry. And they welcome overnighters.

A couple of miles south of the **Chetco River Bridge** an older red-and-white house overlooks Highway 101 from a pastoral hill setting. This is the **Chetco Valley Historical Society Museum** and well deserves time spent exploring the artifacts it harbors.

The house itself was serving as a stagecoach way station and trading post before Abraham Lincoln became president, owned and operated by pioneer law officer Harrison Blake.

The building is filled now with furnishings and tools, and mementos of pioneer times similar to those found in small museums everywhere: a spinning wheel, old sewing machines, a small trunk made in 1706 brought around Cape Horn; plus a collection of Indian relics — baskets and arrowheads and an ancient dugout canoe.

There are even some Japanese swords, recalling the area's claim to being the only spot on the United States mainland to come under aerial attack during World War II. On September 9, 1942, a Japanese plane dropped fire bombs a few miles east of Brookings with minimal damage, although it was judged at the time to have been a retaliation raid for General Doolittle's raid on Tokyo.

By far the most exciting exhibit, however, is an iron casting of a woman's face, fragile and flaking from years of exposure to sand and sea. At least one Northwest author has made a plausible case for its being a relic left by Sir Francis Drake at his still unidentified landfall on the North Pacific Coast during his journeys in 1579.

The mask, discovered on Lone Ranch Beach in 1957, might well be an image of Drake's patroness Queen Elizabeth of England. Certainly it depicts a woman of a century long gone, and certainly it is far older than the earliest colonists' arrival at this place on the Northwest Coast.

The museum is open on winter weekends from 9:00 am to 5:00 pm, Friday through Sunday; on summer afternoons from noon until 5:00 pm. But the attendant lives nearby and has, upon occasion, obliged visitors by opening the museum during off hours.

On the hill near the short flight of stairs which lead up from the highway grows the National Champion Cypress Tree, verified as the world's largest. The tree — ninety-nine feet tall with a spread of over one hundred feet and a trunk more than twenty-seven feet in circumference — shelters a pair of resident owls who have lived there for years.

The grounds surrounding the museum, part of the Pedriolli Brothers Ranch until the house was donated to the Historical Society in 1970, offers an opportunity to stretch legs while returning for an hour or so to an earlier, more romantic and probably less hectic era; as interesting to adults as to children.

One of the most tranquil spots on the southern Oregon coast is **Azalea State Park** just outside the city limits of Brookings. This beautiful hillside setting where the main events of the annual Memorial Day weekend Azalea Festival are held stands out as an oasis of loveliness in an area where natural beauty is routine.

The park is literally filled with azaleas of all sizes, from low borders to tree-shrubs twenty feet or more in height. Some are over three hundred years old. The azaleas bloom from April through June, but even when the blossoms are not splashing pastel free-form designs against the background of shiny green foliage, the shrubs and trees and paths and glens of the park afford a pleasant place for a picnic.

Sheltered spaces are centered with tables of myrtlewood made of planks four inches thick, the grainings and color shadings highlighted by layers of protective coating. Built by members of the Civilian Conservation Corps during the 1930's, each table required a half dozen men to set it in place. A covered shelter has electric stoves and sinks for those who favor a cookout. A stone gazebo at one high spot invites strollers to rest and view the breathtaking spectacle of acres of delicate blooms in late spring.

A natural amphitheater banked by gentle slopes has a stage from which the Azalea Festival Queen and her court are presented. The annual parade, drawing thousands of spectators and hundreds of participants, also ends here.

The festival weekend is filled with events and exhibits to keep visitors in a festive frame of mind. The problem for many may be to find time to take in everything. There are art shows and flower shows; a book sale and a flea market; an old-time fiddlers contest, square dancing, and a waterball tournament; an Air Festival and a Hill Climb; a community church service on Sunday and a Memorial Service on Monday during which wreaths are cast into the harbor in memory of those lost at sea. Purchase of a weekend ticket covers a seafood luncheon and a beef barbecue — both held at the park.

Azalea State Park provides a fitting background for this celebration, memorable among coast events for over forty years. A well-marked exit from Highway 101 at the south end of Brookings takes visitors onto Park Road and to the entrance of the park.

Eight miles up the Northbank Road along the Chetco River is **Loeb State Park** with picnic facilities among a large grove of myrtlewood trees. Loeb Park encompasses one of the finest stands of this beautiful evergreen tree, which grows only in Coos and Curry Counties in Oregon, and in Palestine in the Holy Land. A redwood grove adjoins the myrtlewoods. Loeb Park is far enough inland to enjoy sunshine even on the foggiest days, and there is excellent swimming and fishing here also.

The Lilies of the Field

Oregon's Curry County at the southwestern corner of the state, together with neighboring Del Norte County in California, produces over ninety percent of the Easter lilies grown in the United States. This million dollar industry began to flourish with the advent of World War II when the bulbs were no longer available from Japan.

Daffodils too are a major crop here; and other nursery specialties include hydrangeas and geraniums as well as commercial versions of the azaleas and rhododendrons which cover the coastal slopes with color during the spring.

Strahm's Lilies at Harbor just south of Brookings is representative of the commercial lily farms in the area. Ruth and Harve Strahm have been growing lilies for over twenty years. The bulbs, which bloom late May through August, are harvested in September. During the winter months — November through March — they are busy packing and mailing orders all over the United States and to many foreign countries. Their bulbs find their way to France, Germany, Canada; they even ship bulbs to Holland. And they receive requests from the Soviet Union now and then.

What sets the Strahms apart is that they specialize in pink lilies — from palest blush to deep fiery red. Many of the names in their catalogue of oriental lilies reflect this emphasis: Pink Bouquet, Blushing Bell, Ruby Jewel strain, Red Dragon, Coralbee, Firebrand, Red Jamboree . . . .

Recently developed are the true deep-red varieties which are just coming into their own. Other colors included in the more than sixty varieties listed in their brochures are white, yellow, gold (shading to browns), and countless combinations of these tones.

The Strahms are friendly and gracious, and welcome visitors to the bulb farm, especially when the blooms spread color over the fields. Even for the casual gardener, the tour is a fascinating experience. Lilies range in size from a foot high to almost twelve feet high, with blooms from six to twelve inches across. The Strahms dispense information on the care and cultivation of lily bulbs, personally and in the literature they have available.

The Pink Lily Farm is easy to find by turning off Highway 101 one mile south of the Chetco Bridge on Benham Lane which curves south onto Oceanview Drive. Once headed in the right direction, signs direct visitors right to the greenhouses, a short drive through a rural area in which flowers flourish.

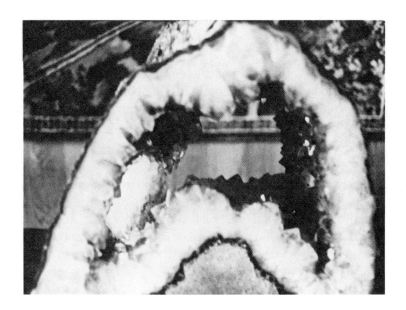

Some Interesting Shops

The **Central Building** at the south end of town houses some shops of interest. **Hamlin's Rocks and Minerals** in the basement is a fairyland of collectors crystals and fossils. Geodes (thundereggs) in magnificent pastel colors — blues and lavenders and frosty white; a chunk of Braziliam amethyst on a rock plate 2½ by 1½ feet in size; cellinite flowers from the bed of an ancient lake near El Paso; fossils of miniscule fish, delicate as Japanese ink drawings; Australian opals set in designer mountings. Hamlin also creates distinctive hand wrought jewelry in gold and silver — rings and bracelets and belt buckles at very reasonable prices.

Nan-El's Treasure Trove on the main floor features quality gifts and coastal arts and crafts; unique jewelry pieces in wood, coral scrimshaw and other natural media; a large selection of exotic shells; plus Oregon wines and specialty foods.

Mory's Arts is a showcase for the paintings of artist Peggy Mory, whose works are shown in collections throughout the country. The other half of the family team is Ralph who handles the custom framing operation at the gallery. Mory's, located north of the city center on Highway 101 where it becomes Chetco Avenue, also carries a complete line of art supplies.

Several interesting shops are located at **Treasure Harbor Village. Driftwood, Etc.** is stocked with handcrafted coastal creations. They will instruct and guide vacationers in collecting and polishing treasures garnered from the beaches. Necessary supplies are available for those who prefer to create their own designs in driftwood.

At **Old Fashioned Fantasies** dolls by the dozens, dressed in hand-crafted costumes will delight children and adults alike. A craft shop, rock shop and an antique store help make this interesting small mall well worth exploring.

Some Thoughts For Food

Flying Gull Restaurant adjacent to the **Brookings Inn** at the north end of town is open from early morning to well past the dinner hour daily, featuring seafoods on their extensive menu. It's a friendly place for every meal.

Jo-Lo's on the highway coming into town from the north is open daily 5:00 am to 7:00 pm; specialties here include homemade pastry and sack lunches for fishing parties and vacationers to carry along with them.

The Coast House features steaks, seafood, and a lengthy wine list for diners.

The Plum Pudding in the Central Building offers a daily special, plus unusual sandwiches on a choice of homemade breads. And the dessert list is enough to make anyone, anywhere renounce dieting forever. The star of their show is the bread basket — a coffee break idea that can't be topped: an assortment of bread samples in a small basket to accompany that rarity of rarities, a mug of hot full-bodied coffee — a perfect ending to any exploration of the Oregon coast!

Annual Events

Azalea Festival — Memorial Day Weekend

Notes:

Index

A

Adobe, The, 108
Agate Beach (Seven Devils Rd.), 148
Agness, 184
d'Aguilar, Commander, 179
Alderhouse II, 64
Allegory Bookshop, 66
Alsea Bay Bridge, 134
Arizona Beach Resort, 172
Astor, John Jacob, 11
Astoria, 11-18
Astoria Column, 12
Astoria Hotel, 14
Astoria Toll Bridge, 16
Aunt Belinda's Salt Water Taffy, 85
Azalea State Park, 198

B

B & C Gallery, 85
Bandon, 156-161
Bandon Art Glass Studio, 156
Bandon Boatworks, 159
Bandon Card & Gift Shop, 157
Bandon Cranberry Festival, 161
Battery Russell, 21
Battle Rock, 165
Battleship Oregon, 16
Bay Bridge Needlework, 90
Bay Front Bakery, 49
Bayocean, 44
Bayside Seafood, 126
Bay Window, 113
Beachcomber Fair, 54
Beach Loop Road (Bandon), 161
Becky Lynn Charters, 176

Ben Holladay, 24
Ben Jones Bridge, 133
Bill's Tavern, 32
Blue Heron French Cheese
    Factory, 50
de Bodega y Quadra, Juan
    Francisco, 179
Boiler Bay Wayside, 70
Bold Duck Sternwheeler, 162
Bostonian, The, 123
Bottom Fishing, 150
Bridge Company, 90
Bridgewater Restaurant, 112
Brookings, 195-203
Brookings Azalea Festival, 198
Bruce's Candy Kitchen, 30

C

Cabrillo, Juan, 177
Calico Kitchen, 94
Cannon Beach, 30-35
Cannon Beach Conference
    Center, 32
Canyon Way Restaurant and
    Bookstore, 86
Cape Arago, 48, 197
Cape Arago Lighthouse, 37
Cape Blanco Lighthouse, 38
Cape Blanco State Park, 173
Cape Foulweather, 67
Cape Gregory Lighthouse, 37
Cape House, The 90
Cape Kiwanda, 46
Cape Meares, 44
Cape Meares Lighthouse, 40
Cape Perpetua, 59
    Campground, 106
    Visitor's Center, 104
Captain Bly's, 128
Captain's Table, 198
Carl G. Washburn State Park,
    106
Catch the Wind Kite Shop, 112
Central Building, 201
Champagne Patio, 88
Charleston, 142-148
Charleston Pottery, 157

Chetco River Coast Guard
    Station, 196
Chetco Travel Trailer Resort, 196
Chetco Valley Historical Society
    Museum, 197
Clark, William, 6, 11
Clear Lake, 100
Cleawox Lake, 100
Coastal Mountain Stables, 117
Coast Range Indian Reservation,
    103
Coast Roast Coffee Co., 66
Coffenbury Lake, 23
Columbia River Maritime
    Museum, 16
Cone, 9, 14
Continental Deli, 96
Cook, Captain James, 37, 68,
    106, 179
Coos Bay, 137-147
Coos Bay (town), 141, 149
Coos-Curry Museum, 138
Coquille Loop Trip, 162
Corps of Discovery, 5
Country Merchant, 158
Coxcomb Hill, 12
Crab Broiler, 25
Cranberry Bogs, 160
Court's White Water Trips, 188

D

Daggatts, 32
D River, 62
Darlingtonia Wayside, 45
Deep Sea Charters, 72
Depoe Bay, 70-75
Depoe Bay Aquarium, 72
Devil's Churn Wayside, 104
Devil's Lake, 62
Devil's Punchbowl, 76
Dick's Seafood, 126
Dolly Wares Doll Museum, 116
Drake, Sir Francis, 42, 146, 177,
    178, 198
Driftwood, Etc., 202
Driftwood Travel Trailer Retreat,
    196

Dunes, The, 99
Dunes Overlook (Florence), 101

E

Ecola State Park, 31
Eel Lake, 100
Egyptian Theatre, 141
Elkton, 123
Embarcadero, The, 84
End of the Jetty, The, 22

F

Face Rock, 156, 161
Fair Winds, 30
Fenton's Farmers Market, 24
Fiddleback Manor, 169
Fisherman's Wharf, 118
Flavel House, 18
Fleet of the Flowers, 75
Florence, 112-119
Flying Gull Restaurant, 202
Fogarty Beach, 71
Fort Astoria, 11
Fort Clatsop, 6-8
Fort George, 12
Fort Stevens State Park, 21
Foxythings Gifts, 74
From Oregon with Love, 167

G

Gardiner, 123
Gardiner Pioneer Cemetery, 124
Garibaldi, 44
Gazebo (Florence), 112
Geppetto's Toy Shoppe, 30
Gold Beach, 183-193
Golden Egg, 191
Golden Hind, The, 144, 177
Golden Storehouse, 142
Gourmet Food Store for Thrifty
    Gourmets, 30
Government Hill, 81, 92
Grant's, 190
Gray, Captain Robert, 180
Gull Gallery, 189

H

Hamlin's Rocks & Minerals, 201
Harbor Light Restaurant, 125
Harbor View Motel, 130
Harrison's Bakery, 25
Hatfield Marine Science Center,
    91
Haystack Rock, 32
Haystack Summer Conference, 34
Heceta, Bruno, 179
Heceta Head Lighthouse, 41
Hilan's Castle, 89
Holiday Charter, 126
Home by the Sea B & B, 167
Honeyman State Park, 100, 121
Horsfall Beach, 100
Hot Pots, 66
House of Books, 141
Hudson Bay Company, 25, 80
Humbug Mountain State Park,
    173

I

Ice Creamery, 30
Incredible Edible Oregon, 113
Indian Creek Recreation Park,
    191
Indian Forest, 115
Indian Trading Post, 115
Indians, 79
Inn at Otter Crest, 68
Inn at Spanish Head, 64
International Burgers & Seafood,
    96
Isaac L. Patterson Bridge, 134

J

Jak's, 90
Jerry's Rogue River Jet Boats,
    188
Jimco Dock, 72
Jo-Lo's, 202
Josephson's Smokehouse, 15
Jot's Resort, 191

K

Kan's, 25
Karla's Krabs, 49
Kirtsis Park, 62
Kitchen Klutter, 113
Knutson's Clocks, 166
Kozy Kove Marina, 97
Kyle & Sons Building, 112

L

La Serre, 108
Lacey's Doll & Antique Museum, 63
Lawrence Gallery, 65
Lewis & Clark Salt Cairn, 26
Lewis, Meriwether, 5
Lightship Columbia, 17
Lincoln City, 61-66
Lincoln County Historical Museum, 89
Little Theater On The Bay, 141
Loeb State Park, 199
Lookout Gift Shop & Observatory, 67, 69
Lucas Ranch, 186

M

McCullough Bridge, 134
Madelaine's B & B, 167
Mapleton Depot, 112
Marhoffer, The, 70
Mariner Square, 86, 87
Mariner Square Gift Shop, 86
Marketplace, The, 65
Marketplace Restaurant, 66
Marshfield Sun Printing Museum, 140
Mary D. Hume, The, 193, 195
Merchant's Beach, 148
Minute Cafe, The, 159
Mo's (Coos Bay), 142
Mo's (Florence), 118
Mo's (Newport), 88
Morning Star II, 51
Morrison's Fireside Restaurant, 32

Mory's Arts, 202
Mosey's Furniture, 96
Muriel O. Ponsler Wayside, 106
Myrtle Burl, 162
Myrtletree, The, 102

N

Nan-El's Treasure Trove, 202
National Champion Cypress Tree, 198
Nature's Wooden Image, 140
Neahkahnie Mountain, 2
Nehalem, 44
Nehalem Bay, 43
Nehalem Bay Trading Co., 47
Nehalem Bay Winery, 49
Neptune Motel, 169
Netarts, 45, 54
Newport, 83-91
Newport Sportfishing, 84
Newport Tradewinds, 84
Norma's, 25
Normandie, 90
North Bend, 137-140
Northpoint Cafe, 74

O

Ocean Foods Market, 15
Oceanside, 45
Old Fashioned Fantastics, 202
Old Trapper Sausage Factory, 50
On Broadway Theater, 141
Once Upon a Breeze, 30
Oregon Dune's National Recreation Area, 126
Oregon Oyster Company, 42
Oswald West State Park, 78
Otter Crest Loop, 67

P

Pacific Brass & Copper Works, 74
Pacific City, 46
Pacific Sands Hometel, 130
Pat's Baskets & Coffees, 31
Pelican's Pouch, 189

Peter Iredale, 21
Phil & Joe's Crab Company, 49
Pier 1 Sportfishing, 72
Pier 11, 14
    Black Murex, 14
    Feedstore Restaurant, 15
Pink Panther Gifts, 74
Pixie Kitchen, 64
Pizza Port, 96
Plum Pudding, The, 203
Pony Village Lodge, 140
Pony Village Mall, 140
Port Orford, 164-169
Posey's Bakery and Cafe, 125
Prehistoric Gardens, 170

R

Raintree Gift & Garden Center, 26
Reedsport, 125
Reedsport Cheese Shoppe, 125
Rhododendron Festival, 119
Riley's on the Rogue, 191
Riverbend Moorage, 42
Road's End Dory Cove, 63
Rogue River Mail Boat Trips, 188
Rogue River, 183

S

Saint Perpetua Trail, 104
Salishan, 65
Salmon Harbor, 127
Salmon Harbor Boat Lift, 126
Sand Dunes Frontier, 120
Sandpiper Gallery, 30
Sandy Camp, 192
Sawdusters, The, 163
Sea Chest, The, 85
Sea Explorers of the Oregon Coast, 177
Sea Fair Gift Shop, 108
Sea Gulch, 93
Sea Gull Charters, 84
Sea Hag, 74
Sea Lion Caves, 110
Sea Ranch Trailer Village, 32
Sea Star Hostel, 159

Seal Rock, 93
Seal Rock Wayside, 93
Seal Rock Art Gallery, 93
Seaside, 24-29
Seaside Aquarium, 26
Seaside Turnaround, 27, 29
Seastrand Plaza, 96
230 Second Street Gallery, 158
Sentinel Building, 162
Seven Devils Road, 148
Seven Seas, 128
Shamrock Charters, 126
Shirley's Country Creations, 108
Shore Acres, 143-146
Siletz Indian Reservation, 81, 92
Singing Springs Resort, 187
Siuslaw River Bridge, 134
Skipanon River Mooring Basin, 19
Smith's Pacific Shrimp Co., 49
South Beach Charters, 91
Southern Oregon Beach Stacks, 181
Sporthaven Park, 196
Sportsman's Cannery, 126
Strahm's Lilies, 200
Stuffed Cubbyhole, 113
Sugar Shoppe, 190
Sunset Bay State Park, 142
Sunset Beach, 144
Surfwood Campground & RV Park, 127
Swafford's Oregon Specialties, 88

T

Tahkenitch Lake, 99
Tenmile Lake, 100
Thistledown, 30
Thomas Creek Bridge, 134
Thompson Charter, 126
Three Gables, 159
Tillamook, 45
Tillamook Bay, 43, 44
Tillamook Cheese Factory, 50
Tillamook County Cheese, Wine Tour, 49

Tillamook County Pioneer Museum, 45
Tillamook Rock Light, 39
'Tis the Season, 30
Toledo Loop Trip, 92
Tole Tree, The, 107
Toy Factory, 114
Tradewinds Trollers, 71
Trail of the Restless Waters, 104
Trail of the Whispering Spruce, 104
Trail's End Marathon, 27
Trident Antiques, 95
Truculent Oyster, The 167
Tu Tu Tun Vacation Lodge, 188

U

Umpqua River Bridge, 133
Umpqua River Light Station, 37
Umpqua River Lighthouse, 41, 130
Underseas Gardens, 85
Up Against the Wall, 65

V

Victory House, 52
Viscaino, Sebastian, 178

W

Waldport, 93-95
Waldport Drugstore, 96
Waldport Yarn & Book Shop, 96

Waldport Town Center Mini Mall, 96
Walter's Landing Leather, 166
Warrenton, 19
Wax Works, The, 86
Weber's Fish Market & Restaurant, 118
Wedderburn, 183
West Coast Game Farm, 163
Westerly Webs, 156
Whale Cove, 75
Whale Memorial Panel, 56
Whales, The, 57
Whale's Tale, The, 86
Whiskey Run Beach, 148
Whiskey Run Silver Shop, 156
White Water Trips, 189
Winchester Bay, 126-130
Winchester Bay Motel, 130
Windward Inn, 117
Windy Cove Campground, 127
Woahink Lake, 99
Wooden Nickel, 165
Wood Gallery, The, 85
Woodsman's Native Nursery, 116

Y

Yachats, 103-109
Yachats Gift Shop, 107
Yachats Pie & Kite Shop, 108
Yaquina Bay Bridge, 133
Yaquina Bay Lighthouse, 38
Yaquina Head Light Station, 38
Young's Bay Plaza, 19